MW01579048

Fighting FOR Democracy

Fighting FOR Democracy

THE TRUE STORY OF JIM HIGGINS (1907-1982)

A Canadian Activist in Spain's Civil War

JIM HIGGINS with Janette Higgins

Copyright © 2020 by Janette Higgins
First Edition — 2020

Janette Higgins is available for readings, book clubs and other events, and school and university visits, either in person or via Skype/Facetime. All enquiries, including rights, should be directed to her at: jimhigginsmemoir@gmail.com

Front Cover: Photograph of Jim Higgins, taken in the late 1930s or early 1940s. By now, his nose had been broken twice in boxing matches.

Back Cover: Image of a small medal found in Jim Higgins's effects. The raised fist was an anti-fascist symbol used by civilians and soldiers alike who supported the Republican side in the Spanish Civil War.

All rights reserved.

No part of this publication may be reproduced in any form, or by any means, electronic or mechanical, including photocopying, recording, or any information browsing, storage, or retrieval system, without permission in writing from FriesenPress.

ISBN
978-1-5255-6694-3 (Hardcover)
978-1-5255-6695-0 (Paperback)
978-1-5255-6696-7 (eBook)

1. Biography & Autobiography, Historical
2. Biography & Autobiography, Military
3. Biography & Autobiography, Social Activists

 FriesenPress

Suite 300 - 990 Fort St
Victoria, BC, V8V 3K2
Canada

www.friesenpress.com

Distributed to the trade by The Ingram Book Company

DEDICATED TO THE MEMORY OF...

...my mother, Reta Palliser, a wise woman who picked a good man,
my father, Jim Higgins, who gave me a gift beyond measure,
and his comrades in Spain of all nationalities.

AND TO TODAY'S YOUNG PEOPLE:

Democracy, world health, and social justice are at stake.
Your activism makes a difference.

CONTENTS

Prologue
A FATHER'S MYSTERIOUS PAST

"Heroes deserve histories, too." This was the last line of a 1980 book review by William French in Canada's *Globe and Mail* newspaper. Leading up to it, he wrote, "It's a lovely story, with only one omission. Jimmy Higgins, the soldier, remains a mystery. Why did he go to Spain? What has happened to him?"

The book French had praised was *The Tall Solder, My 40-year Search for the Man who Saved My Life*. It was written by Manuel Alvarez, and captured his experience as a boy growing up in the Spanish Civil War (SCW). But more than that, it told of his quixotic quest to find the man who had saved his life in 1938 in Corbera d'Ebre, Spain, in the midst of fascist bombing.

A shell had hit the town's water tank, and the torrent it unleashed carried eleven-year-old Manuel to certain death down a rocky hill. Badly injured, he was suddenly pulled out and carried on the back of a soldier to a first-aid station. Manuel survived and vowed to his father that he would find that soldier to thank him. All he knew was that the man was Canadian.

Manuel pursued leads in Spain, but all was for naught, and by the late 1950s, he had emigrated to Vancouver. Still, it seemed hopeless. He could find little information about the Canadians who had volunteered to fight in the Spanish Civil War, other than that they were in the Mackenzie-Papineau Battalion, and were known as "Mac-Paps." It was almost as if they never existed.

Growing up in Peterborough, Ontario as one of Jim Higgins's five children, I knew only that he'd had a rough time during the Great Depression, and I'd had some vague idea about him fighting in the Spanish Civil War. I saw him active in his union and excited to work on Walter Pitman's 1960 campaign when the New Party—a precursor to the New Democratic Party—ran in a Peterborough by-election.

I had wondered at some of the things he was passionate about. He was always writing letters to the editor of the *Peterborough Examiner*. I remember one about the low wages earned by nurses: during one of his hospital stints, he'd been dismayed to discover that nurses earned less than a janitor. Another outlined his argument for community colleges, including one for Peterborough. Young people needed to be taught skills that prepared them for work. I found it curious. Where did these convictions come from?

I also caught glimpses of a secret past. What was the meaning of the beat-up brown leather jacket that hung in his carpentry workshop? There were allusions to the Spanish Civil War. Did he take it off a dead soldier? Just what was the Spanish Civil War, and how had he been involved?

I never knew my father to be a swimmer, but as a young child, I remember being alarmed one Sunday when we were splashing about in a lake. Dad slipped under the water and seemed to disappear. Where was he? Did he drown? He was under for so long. Finally, to my relief, he surfaced quietly some distance away. Not breathing hard. Not snorting water. No one else did that. What was that all about? It never happened again.

He also once told me that he had biked across the United States, starting from the West Coast. He was headed to New York City but stopped in Ohio. Where did he go next? Was this just a lark? I thought it was—until I settled down to work on his memoir and learned the real reason. It was no lark.

Another time, he told me that on the ship that brought him back from the Spanish Civil War, he'd been invited to sit at the captain's table. More than once. Why would my factory-worker father receive such an invitation? Didn't you have to be wealthy and connected?

Then there was the painting. One day—I must have been seven or eight—I was under the cellar stairs where my mother's preserves were neatly lined up on shelves for the winter. My father was an amateur oil painter, and hidden away in a cranny were some paintings. I pulled them out.

There were the usual landscapes and still-lifes, but among them was one I'd never had the nerve to ask about and never saw again. It was of a woman, dead on the ground with a cat licking the blood pooling around her. Why had he painted such a disturbing image?

It was years later, at Christmas 1976, that all five of us children prevailed upon him to write about his life before we knew him. By then, he was seventy years old and for twenty-five years had been dealing with chronic pain after the failure of two major back surgeries.

It took a while to realize he had taken us seriously. In fact, throughout 1977, he wrote prodigiously in pencil on legal-size foolscap, using volunteer and paid typists to type what he had written.

Then, in early September 1977, the Mackenzie-Papineau veterans' group encouraged surviving veterans to write about their time in Spain. Of course, my father had just written a bunch. He sent it in and continued writing.

Coincidentally, a month later, a feature article about the Canadian volunteers who fought in the Spanish Civil War was distributed across Canada in the *Weekend Magazine*. It was written by Eve Drobot and titled *The Soldiers in $8 Suits*.

A man in Vancouver read Drobot's article with mounting excitement: a Spanish immigrant named Manuel Alvarez. He tracked down Lionel Edwards, a local Mac-Pap veteran quoted in the article, and told him of his quest to find the Canadian who had saved his life.

It was not promising. There had been close to 1,700 Canadian volunteers in the Spanish Civil War, and there was so little to go on. Besides, more than 400 had been killed. Lionel Edwards, who himself had no idea who it could be, contacted a vet in Toronto.

It turned out that Edwards' Toronto contact had just read the material recently submitted by my father. The shortest piece, written almost as an afterthought, was about rescuing a boy after a fascist bomb hit a water tank. The last line was, "I don't suppose the lad could have survived."

The search was over. Incredibly, and against all odds, Manuel Alvarez had found his saviour. Oh, both were sceptical; that is until they actually met in spring 1978 and verified that Jim Higgins was in Corbera d'Ebre on the date of the rescue, and nailed down other details that only they could know.

SO, IN ANSWER TO William French, the hero did have a history. In fact, after my father died, I learned he had written half of his Spanish Civil War material in 1939. As for the rest of his memoir, written in 1977, he was close to the end of his life and only able to do rewrites on some of it. He knew it needed major editing and made that clear in ad libs while audiotaping his manuscript. In 2017, I listened to those tapes for the first time as I embarked on my quest to bring a hero's history into the light.

A proud daughter,
Janette Higgins

Introduction
GREENWICH VILLAGE,
NEW YORK, 1940

RETA PALLISER, MY WIFE and partner, knew me better than anyone. Most, including my children, knew very little. There was one exception—an artist I met in New York at a Greenwich Village art gallery in 1940.

I felt his presence while studying a portrait titled, Unknown. It reminded me of people I had met; I even saw something of myself in it.

My thoughts were interrupted, "You seem to have an intense interest in that painting." He introduced himself as the artist and invited me to join him for coffee.

I learnt that he had previously made his living by painting portraits that flattered. This one was meant to capture a person's character. I was interested in his thoughts on non-conformity, and in turn, he seemed very interested in my past. Coffee lingered on to dinner. As we were leaving the restaurant, a train on the elevated tracks rumbled overhead.

"What were your thoughts when the train was making all that noise?" he asked.

I told him that I would dislike living a few feet from the train.

"Why 'dislike' instead of 'hate'?" he responded.

I told him I would only use "hate" in the most extreme circumstances. He seemed to understand the distinction.

When we parted, he said, "You mention going back to Canada soon. I'd like to know more about you." He asked if I would call him each morning. I agreed.

While walking back to my room on the Lower East Side, a little over two miles, I sensed that our talk was bringing to mind buried parts of my life. Later that evening, I recalled a run-in I'd had with a tractor on a prairie farm in 1930. All the details flooded back.

When I phoned the artist the next morning, he said he thought I might not call—that I had seemed withdrawn. "That's why I didn't ask you for your address."

He added, "And I have a notion that the name you used was not your own."

"That's correct, but how did you guess?"

"It wasn't purely guesswork. Do you remember taking off your coat yesterday and slinging it across your shoulder?"

I did. It was when we were leaving the restaurant. Underneath, I had been wearing a short-sleeve shirt.

"Would you care to tell me why you had H. J. Higgins tattooed on your left arm?"

He went on, "You told me your name was Jim Henderson."

"Are you a detective?" I retorted.

"Now ease up. I am an artist. I observe the world around me." I relaxed a bit.

The artist wanted to know more about my life. I told him I had been born in London, England and orphaned during the Great War. He interrupted me with a probing question, one of many that sparked our conversations over the next several weeks. He would come to know much about me, including when and why I would use the word "hate." I may even have told him I was in New York to escape heat from the Royal Canadian Mounted Police.

I am writing this in my seventieth year at the request of my children. In letting go of my stories and secrets, released by memories of the artist's probing those many years ago, I am hoping they will better understand me. Perhaps others will be interested as well.

Jim Higgins
Peterborough, Ontario, Canada
1977

Chapter 1
ORPHANED

I WAS BORN JULY 26, 1907, without aid of a midwife, in the attic of a pub run by my parents. The address was 644 Wandsworth Road, Clapham, London, England, and the name on my birth certificate was Harry James Thomas Higgens.[1]

Throughout my life, I have used variations on this name for reasons that will become evident by the time my story ends. It is now 1977, and though I am writing in my seventieth year, details of my past are surfacing as if they happened yesterday.

My first memory is of my two sisters swinging me back and forth on an iron gate while I held on tightly to avoid falling off. Their black straw hats were freshened up with what smelt like shoe polish. I also remember rough rides over cobblestone streets on the handle bars of my father's bike. They were called "bone shakers" for good reason.

The streets were always busy. There were blackened chimney sweeps, coal men with carts who hoisted sacks of coal on their backs to deliver to houses, and the gas-lamp lighters who carried long poles to put the street lamps on and off. "Knocker ups" also had long poles, but theirs were used to tap on the upper windows of the workers early in the morning to wake them. Milkmen, with horse-drawn wagons, used pint measures to dip milk out of large cans into jugs held by waiting customers. Other horses—Belgians, Clydesdales, and Percherons—drew plows and beer wagons.

Then everything changed. Britain was in the middle of the First World War and during a German Zeppelin raid over London my father was killed.[2] My memory is blank until I found myself in an orphanage where I was told I had been in hospital for some time. I was seven or eight.

When I questioned them later, even my sisters could not tell me the reason I was hospitalized. All they knew was that, one day, a person had spoken to my mother, who had become seriously ill after my father's death, and that I did not return home that evening.

I later learnt that my mother was unable to provide for my two sisters and myself, which is why we were sent our separate ways. I was told that my mother had a small pension and was renting a cottage on an estate in southern Wales where she lived with a companion.

I REMEMBER THE ORPHANAGE very well. It was a large house set on two or three acres with an orchard. A stone wall surrounded the property and entry was through double iron gates. When I arrived, the matron informed me of the rules and said I would be there until a place was found for me.

There were six bedrooms; one for the matron, four for us eight boys who slept two to a room, and the sixth for the teacher who filled in as a nurse and looked after our scrapes.

The orphanage is one of the highlights of my life. After sixty years, I can still feel the love in that house. We were not coddled, but it was almost as though we still had parents. Among the staff was a cook, a jolly plump woman with a twinkle in her eye, a person one could admire and respect. The kitchen was spotless and smelt of cooking and freshly baked bread. Although the kitchen was off limits, the cook would always invite one of us to "help" for a few minutes. This was rewarded with a cookie or small cake.

The cook's assistant was made of sterner stuff. She took over when the cook had a day off, and there were no treats. There was also a maid who made the beds, cleaned the bedrooms, and waited on the tables.

The person I remember most fondly was Mr. Brown, the gardener. By chance, I learnt that his first name was Harry. Besides looking after the grounds, he was the gatekeeper and lived in the one-room stone gatehouse. I was there one day when the bell sounded. He opened the gates for a man delivering meat who left saying, "See you at the pub this evening, Harry."

Mr. Brown interceded when the matron confronted me because my knees were stained green. We boys wore short pants, called knickers, which ended just above the knees, and I had knelt on the grass while helping Mr. Brown weed a flowerbed. Matron asked him why he had not stopped me from kneeling and getting dirty. Mr. Brown's words were, in effect, "Don't blame the lad, as he is a constant companion of mine who seems to be very interested in gardening." The matron suggested that, in future, he get me a sack to kneel on.

Harry Brown taught me many things and made me notice what was happening around me. The most memorable thing I learnt was not to be afraid of honeybees. He would spread moistened sugar over his arm and put it in the flowerbed. Bees climbed all over his arm but he was never stung.

Later in life, while people watched, I would let honey bees crawl over my face, keeping my mouth closed and a finger blocking my nostrils. Then I would gently brush them off. They never stung me either. I thought then, and still do now, that Harry Brown was my first real friend.

I particularly remember the entertaining escapades of some local boys during apple season. Half a dozen of them would climb the stone wall and start scrumping—stealing apples. I do not recall a telephone in the orphanage, but somehow the local policeman would arrive at the scene.

We orphanage boys watched with amusement from the second storey windows as the culprits scrambled over the stone wall, their jackets loaded with apples, all the while thumbing their noses at the cop.

We were also taken on excursions in a covered horse-drawn carriage with five seats on each side. One time, we went to a farm where the farmer introduced us to his pigs, horses, and cattle, and let us pick apples. Another time, we went to boat races, which we watched from a bridge. Occasionally, someone well off would take us for a walk and buy us treats at a sweet shop. Those little things meant so much to me.

At some point, I was taken by train to Manchester. My escort, probably a social worker, had a lunch basket with bread and jam, an orange, and an earthenware bottle of ginger beer.

I was delivered to the Ardwick Industrial School, the initials of which were used in the motto, "Able, Industrious, and Sober." The documents of my past arrived with me, including the addresses of my mother and two sisters. It was a boarding school for boys eight to sixteen years old, and like me, most were wards of the government. We made everything we wore—suits and coats in the tailor shop and shoes in the shoemaker shop.

Two cooks taught some of us how to do things in the kitchen. Vegetables were cooked in steamers, as was the oatmeal for breakfast. Two large ovens were used to roast meat and bake bread. One oven could hold twenty loaves. We even grew our own vegetables. Most of the boys did not like weeding, but I enjoyed it.

School ran from eight a.m. to four p.m., with an hour off for lunch. After lessons, we spent two hours a day at our trades. I picked carpentry, and made and repaired the dining hall tables. I also learnt carving and cabinet making.

We could choose our own extra-curricular activities. I became a member of the band and showed enough talent in the boxing club to be nicknamed "Boxer." I was also a member of the Manchester Swimming Team. At five every weekday morning, I was awakened by the night watchman and would go off to the public swimming pool to practise for an hour.

Every Saturday morning, the "good boys" were given an allowance and often played football on the commons. The lads who had misbehaved were given kitchen work like preparing potatoes. Down in the cellar was a potato peeling machine, a contraption somewhat like a cement mixer with a spiked interior. A bag of raw spuds was dumped into it along with water. The boys turned handles at each end to rotate the container. After a few minutes, it was opened and the spuds were drained. The only thing left for the boys to do was remove the eyes before the potatoes were cooked.

After the noon meal, the lads who got through the week without causing trouble were given passes to various activities. Some went to the silent movies—flickers—and if either of Manchester's professional soccer teams was playing, we were escorted to the stadium and let in for free.

During the week, when we were allowed out for an hour or so each evening, we would go "butting," which meant picking up cigarette butts on the curbs. We would salvage the tobacco and make hand-rolled cigarettes. I was ten or so when I started smoking.

But all was not milk and honey. There were times I had the "blues" ... times when I saw a lad with his father at a footfall match and would feel like crying, though I did not of course. Boys were not supposed to do such a sissy thing. And when I look back, I feel that even though my father was killed, I did have a family, but we were split up, preventing any sort of family life.

I was not an angel in any sense and was often in trouble. I am stubborn by nature and at times thought the whole world was against me. I think I used to break the rules just to be punished. Though I liked most of the people in charge of my welfare, I was a rebel. While physical punishments such as caning and birching may not have worked, my guardians soon found I was very cooperative with any threat of removal from extra-curricular activities.

There was one master who had been in the school for only three months: a pure sadist named Mr. Dunbar, who used the cane for minor offences. Everybody was afraid of him. One day, he heard me whispering and ordered me to the front as he reached for his cane. He lectured us on the need for discipline, and then asked me why I had been talking. I told him I was not talking, I was whispering. He got riled and shouted, "When I ask a question, I want you to say 'sir'!"

He held up the cane, and with all his force, started hitting my hands, cutting them. After every two hits, he demanded that I say "sir." I remained silent, no whimpering, as he gave me twelve whacks, six on each hand. Finally, he gave up and ordered me to the infirmary. The ten boys were very quiet. As I left, he said, "The next time you will say 'sir' or else you can expect the same treatment."

I promised myself that, before he caned me again, I would take that cane and hit him across the face, regardless of the consequences. I felt completely degraded. I went to the nurse who immediately took me to the school office. Without saying a word, she lifted up my bloody hands.

Mr. Kelly, the superintendent, demanded to know who was responsible. I replied, "Mr. Dunbar, sir."

We never saw that sadist teacher again, and I became a hero to the boys. To this day, I am one of those guys who will not be pushed around.

Another of the staff, though not close to being a sadist, was called "bloody bastard" behind his back. He would get his kicks from sneaking up in tennis shoes and catching us smoking in the WC. (In those days, bathrooms were called water closets, or WCs.) One day, he put ashes on a frozen slide we had made. We plotted our revenge.

His main job was to make sure we were all in bed, so we decided our prank would take place in the dorm. All twenty of us dorm mates were in on it. We planned to use sand and water. It suited the offense, and besides, there were fire pails under each window, some filled with sand and others with water. It was important, though, that nothing appear to be missing from the pails.

The problem was solved earlier in the day by filling all the sand buckets right to the top. Then two of the boys snuck a ladle and empty pail from the kitchen. We loaded the ladle with sand by taking a little from each sand pail and filled the empty pail with water from the WC.

It was a cold night, below freezing. The dormitories were on the third floor, and ours was directly over the path of our tormentor as he made his rounds. We posted a lookout at a window near the far end of our dorm. When he signaled, we knew the master was under our window. The ladle of sand was thrown onto the man's head, and when he looked up, a pail of water hit him square in the face.

By the time he had climbed the two flights of stairs to our dormitory, we had hidden the empty water bucket and were all "asleep." He turned on the lights and checked the fire buckets. All was in order. He checked the towels that were hung on the heads of our beds to see if any were damp. Nothing there either. Discouraged, he left to finish his rounds. Nothing was said about the incident, but we noticed that sand and ashes were no longer spread on our slide.

I must mention that the school was not a reform institution, and that the youngsters were not committed by magistrates as unruly children; it was for boys like myself who had lost parents during the First World War.

We were often visited by the Member of Parliament and the mayor and councilmen of Manchester, and women's groups helped on holidays like Christmas. They took over on December 24th and prepared our Christmas dinner under the direction of the cook and his assistant.

On Christmas Day, there was a magician, a concert that included singing, and a magic lantern show with slides projected on a screen. Afterwards, we received presents. Through the next week we were taken to all kinds of activities. One of the most popular was the pantomime. This was also a time when relatives visited to take us out for a meal and a show. I had two aunts and uncles who took me out, and I learnt more about what had happened to my parents and sisters.

Around the age of twelve, I was presented with a life-saving medal for rescuing a six-year-old girl who had fallen into the canal. While others watched and did nothing, I jumped in fully clothed and brought her to the embankment where helping hands lifted us out.

I did not think anything of it. I was a strong swimmer, and as far as I was concerned, it could have been an everyday affair. The canal was only fourteen feet wide, and at no time was I in any trouble, but the person who presented the award spoke of my having done it at risk to my own life.

Those early years set the tone of my life. I felt secure, yet always had a sense of something off kilter, that my life was unpredictable. It was something I had to control, overcome, or accept.

I was thought to be an outstanding student in academics and sports, as well as in my carpentry trade, and at the age of thirteen was taken to a school in Bristol with a refined name I cannot remember. Soon after, I learnt from my older sister, Kate, that my mother had died.

The school was small, only twenty boys. It was situated at the top of a hill above a natural ravine by the river, with houses on the street below. Across the street was a shipyard that operated twenty-four hours a day, keeping me awake at night until I adjusted to the noise.

There were steps down to a gatehouse at the street where we each had a card. We did not need permission to leave, but when we did, we put our card in the "out" file. On return, we changed it to the "in" file—a precaution meant to account for everybody, especially in case of fire.

Six of us trained at the cabinet shop in the school. The rest went to assorted trade shops in the city on weekday afternoons. They learnt shorthand, clerking, cooking, plumbing, and steam engineering. Two went to a military officer training school.

It was in the cabinet shop that I learnt to make furniture without nails using only dovetail, dowels, and hand carving. The cutting was done by hand saws, and the legs were made on treadle lathes operated with our feet. The furniture was custom made for people who ordered from our instructors. Although we were only six in the class, we were taught by a master cabinet maker and his assistant.

I joined the boxing club, and my Boxer nickname stuck. I was also accepted into the Bristol Swimming Club and received another life-saving award. This time it was for saving a boy who sank in the oil-slicked river near the shipyard. I have always thought that the people who trained me deserved these awards.

A town councilman became friendly with me when he attended a citywide swimming tournament. Some eighty boys in my age group took part, and over four days, all but six of us were eliminated. The final race was a hundred yard sprint. I came in third.

The councilman's name was John Jackson. He had been a captain in the First World War and was taking care of an orphaned Belgian girl, Lucy, whom he had brought back to England as his ward. He picked me up Saturday afternoons and would take me and Lucy out for picnics in the country, usually to his farmer friends.

Impressed upon my memory is the first time I had a real sexual experience. I was about fifteen. I had had sex with girls my own age, but it was the usual groping, and sometimes more, while standing in some dark corner.

This time it was the real thing. Lucy had enticed me (this is not a lie) into a barn loft, and we made love in the hay while the men were out shooting rabbits. To say we had a ball was to put it mildly. When her foster father returned, we were quarrelling and insulting each other as before.

When I graduated, the school helped me find a job in a carpentry shop, where I was given a broom and told to keep the place clean. I am pretty sure I knew more than the people working there and either quit or was let go. Probably let go. Then I worked in a glass factory, but there was no safety protection, and I quit when I saw a piece of glass shatter and blind a young chap.

Out of work, I went to an agency and was asked if I wanted to go to sea, which I thought would be wonderful. I went to a marine school for six months, learnt to read a compass, and got training on longboats and a sailing ship. When I was finished, they gave me a waterfront address to go to for a job as a cabin boy on a tramp steamer.

This would have suited me, because tramps went all over the world visiting various ports. It would be an adventure. As I was about to walk up the gangplank, I saw a crowd around two guys who were fighting with knives. I went no further. Besides, it was a rusty old hulk that had not been painted since it was new. I went back to the marine school with my story, but they "suggested" I look for a job on my own.

I got a couple of short-term jobs, including one on a farm, but was let go when the busy season was over. I went to the authorities again, and this time they asked me if I would like to go to either Australia or Canada. By now, my two sisters were in Canada, so it was what I chose.

I was told my passage would be paid if I worked at least one season harvesting wheat on the prairies. I agreed. To qualify, I was sent to a farm in South Wales where I learnt to milk cows and plow the land using a horse-drawn hand plow.

Four months later, I was on my way to Canada.

Chapter 2
BOOM, THEN BUST

I WILL NEVER FORGET my arrival in Canada.[3] It was August 1928, and I had just turned twenty-one. About thirty of us were in a cement-floored room being questioned by government bureaucrats who were deciding where we would be sent. We were chatting on rows of wooden benches, and a uniformed guard kept ordering us to stop talking. We thought this was unreasonable so we ignored him.

Then one of the men lit a cigarette and the guard shouted, "Put that cigarette out!" We rose off the benches and surrounded the guard, voicing our displeasure. An officer was brought in to escort the smoker out. At this point, I let the officer know that, if one of us was removed, the rest would leave with him. The guards had a brief exchange, and then told us to keep calm and smoke if we wished—an empty remark since, by then, we were all smoking anyway.

I was assigned to a small town in Saskatchewan and put on a steam train called the "Harvester Special." I enjoyed harvesting and made good friends. At sunup, we headed out to the fields with a horse-drawn wagon loaded with thrashing equipment, returning after sundown. When the harvest was over, I had worked off my passage to Canada.

I fell in love with the country and its people of all races and creeds. Canada at that time had a population of only ten or so million. Such a large expanse with so few people! I easily found carpentry work and had dreams of homesteading in Alberta with the money I saved.

Hardly a year later, in late October 1929, the stock market crashed. I was working in Regina for Carter, Hall, and Hellinger Construction with a ten-man carpentry crew. The foreman, who was responsible for about forty men, was assisted by one or two straw bosses who did the same work as the crews —finishing the insides of new buildings—but who were paid a little more for setting the pace and keeping the rest of us in line.

We worked Monday to Friday, from seven in the morning to seven at night, with a half-hour break for lunch. On Saturdays, we worked from seven to four and collected our pay after.

In the spring of 1930, our wages were reduced by thirty percent. Within a short time, we were hit with another cut. I protested but was told I was lucky to be working, and that there were many who would be happy to take my place. After the third cut, the foreman and I were the only ones left of the original ten.

One Saturday, when I was handed my pay envelope, the girl asked if I was married. I told her I was not, and as a joke, asked if she would like a date. It was no joke. She told me that single men were being replaced by married men, and I was told not to report for work on Monday. That was the way most non-unionized were treated: informed one day, out of a job the next. There was no place a worker could turn to for help.

When I applied for other jobs, the first two questions were "Where did you last work?" and "Why were you dismissed?" I would then be told to come back in a week. It became apparent that the real reason I was fired was not because I was single but because I had been trying to unionize the workers. This information was obviously passed on to potential employers, because when I went back later, I would be told that the job was already taken. In this way, agitators and union organizers were kept out of the labour force.

After a month or so of job hunting, a friend told me that the government employment office had my name on a "do not employ" list. I had a hard time believing this, so we hatched a plan. While I was in the employment office being interviewed, my friend started a row in the waiting room. It worked. My interviewer left his office for a few minutes, which gave me time to check the drawer I had seen him open when I came in. It was true. I had been blacklisted. This meant I would not be able to find a job in my trade.

I spoke about these problems at a Trade Union Council meeting, and it was suggested I organize unskilled workers. I found a job with a road-building contractor spreading a mix of tar, sand, and gravel. The weather was hot, and within three days, the tar fumes had burnt my skin. I would not have minded so much if the workers had not kept their distance when I suggested we organize. Only one worker agreed with me: another Englishman named Bill. He was about six feet tall and weighed over two hundred pounds. He was strong and could work hard like myself.

Within a week, the foreman handed us our pay and told us we were both fired, because we were a couple of trouble makers. Bill was about to strike the foreman when I pulled him away and pointed to a nearby cop. We turned in our rakes and shovels and retired to a pub where Bill said he felt like rubbing the bastard's face in the hot tar.

After another useless visit to a Labour Council meeting, I took Bill to a meeting of a political group I belonged to.[4] In return, Bill took me to his Communist Party cell. We got nowhere with those "armchair generals."

Frustrated and disillusioned, Bill and I left it all behind and went to England. After six weeks of living it up on the two thousand dollars I had in savings, I came back to Canada with little left. I was certain I would get a job in my trade. After all, it had been two years since the stock market crashed, and according to the politicians, "prosperity was just around the corner."

My first stop was Toronto. I had no luck finding a job there, so I headed west to Regina by train. Maybe I would find work there. When I arrived at noon, it was completely dark with a dust storm raging. I was lucky to find a hotel near the train station. Crop prices were already depressed, and now with the dust storm, many farmers' crops would be destroyed. Finding a job might not be so easy.

I did get work as a lifeguard in Regina and went into the lake twice when people got into trouble, but otherwise it was boring. I decided to try my luck in Alberta and dug into my savings to buy a Model T Ford from a man named Joe. He had been unemployed for a while and asked if he could join me when I told him I was going to Alberta. As it turned out, I drove him all the way to his family's farm near Cranbrook, British Columbia.

Before we left Regina, I bought a spare tire, two new tubes, a tire-repair kit with pump, and extra gas that we kept in a couple of cans tied to the running boards. We also bought canned beans, bully beef, and other food that would keep.

The first day's journey across flat prairie was uneventful, and we pulled into a farm before dark, having spotted one with a woodpile. We offered to split and stack the wood in exchange for a meal and a "bed" in the hayloft. This worked other nights as well. We replenished our water containers and were usually sent on our way with a packed lunch and vegetables from the farmer's garden.

I stayed with Joe's family briefly, sold the Model T to his parents, and worked for short periods with local farmers. When the harvest was about to start, I jumped a freight train back to Alberta and got off at Pincher Creek. A man came up and asked if I could drive a tractor, and I said I could. He took me for a meal, and as in most small prairie towns, the restaurant was run by Chinese. You could always get good food at a reasonable price. A steak dinner with coffee and a slice of pie cost less than fifty cents.

He wanted to make sure I could handle his tractor—a Massey Harris—so we went to his farm. It was set on 1280 level acres with a full view of the blue-grey Rockies, their tops white with snow reflecting the sun. It was a beautiful and peaceful scene that I can see in my mind's eye today.

The tractor was a giant. The rear wheels were about six feet in diameter and two feet wide. It had a small five-gallon gasoline tank used for starting and a large kerosene tank to which the operator would switch for field work.

I had to use two hands to crank the large handle one complete turn at a time and I learnt it could take anywhere from three to twenty of these individual cranks to get it started. With a Model T Ford, you could turn the crank handle six or more revolutions at a time, but if the operator tried something like that with this monster, and it backfired, he could end up about twenty feet from the machine with a broken arm.

I climbed the rungs welded to the rear and took the seat, which rested on a half inch thick steel platform. Its top speed was a little more than four miles an hour, but what it lacked in speed, it made up in power. Its normal load was eight plows. Behind them was a hitch of the same width holding disk harrows for breaking up the plowed earth. The length of the area to be worked was half a mile to a mile long, in strips a quarter mile apart.

Seeing I could handle the tractor, the farmer told me I had a job for at least two months. At supper that night, he told me that he had bought the farm only two years before. He had been a banker in Toronto, but found it stressful, and had come west on his doctor's advice. Being manager of a bank during the Depression would have been stressful for anyone with a conscience.

While I was there, another farmer's barn burned to the ground. He had insurance, so was able to buy the lumber to rebuild it, but it would have taken a long time, so each day different neighbours helped him out. I rode one of my employer's horses over on evenings or on days when it was too damp to combine the crop. Using an adz and broad axe, I squared logs for the foundation and beams for the loft.

At the end of harvest, while I was plowing the wheat stubble under, the tractor suddenly increased speed, then lost power. The radiator was sending off clouds of steam, and thinking it was about to blow up, I stopped and unscrewed the cap. This was not the thing to do.

The pressurized steam escaped and flattened me six feet in front of the tractor. I had been wearing dust goggles so my eyes were not injured, but they closed to slits because of the swelling caused by the scald. I lost a layer of skin and could not shave for some time.

I worked hard and put in long hours but was always invited to join the family when they went to Pincher Creek for movies and shopping. It is one of my fondest memories of the Depression, because that family treated me as their son.

Just before I left, my boss contracted for me, and some of his horses, to work on provincial road building for three weeks on a road allowance through his land. My job was to drive sixteen horses pulling a three-gang plow—a wooden plow frame with three blades. It was challenging work, but I enjoyed it.

I was offered other jobs in the area, but took an offer elsewhere in Alberta to work with horses. I have always been attracted to animals, but I especially liked horses.

Chapter 3
HORSE SENSE

THE FIRST TIME I worked with wild horses, I used nothing but gut instinct. Those around me "broke" a horse's spirit using force and violence. I respected the animals too much to break them. I called what I did "gentling."

I had already gentled many horses by the time I got a job with Joe Mason, who had a ranch at the foot of the Canadian Rockies. I had been referred by a horse trader who told Joe that I was one of the best.

It took two afternoons to get acquainted with the ranch, which had 4,000 acres and about 500 wild horses. When they were rounded up once a week to check for ailments, a roan mare led the string, which was unusual, since it is usually a stallion that leads. On the second afternoon, we found a horse with a broken leg, and the rancher was forced to shoot it. It was an act of mercy.

When we arrived back at the house, Joe called someone who picked up dead animals. I had heard only that they were taken to the glue factory, but Joe told me there was more to it than that. Yes, the hooves were used for making glue, but the animals were skinned for their hides, their bones ground into meal, and if the horse had not died from disease, the meat could be sold.

One day, Joe told me he would like the roan mare tamed for riding. "Will you try the job without breaking her spirit?" One of his sons had mistreated the mare, and she was wary of humans. I asked if there was a time limit. "No," he said, "take your time, and if you use your spare time, I'll give you extra pay."

The next day, three of us cut the mare out and put her in a small corral. That evening, with Joe watching, I spent an hour or so walking around the outside of the corral. Every time I approached the fence, the mare bared her teeth and rolled her eyes. I spoke quietly, "Okay, sweetheart, I'm not going to hurt you. I just want to be friends." The rancher overheard me, and her name became "Sweetheart."

The second day, nobody but myself fed Sweetheart. I fed her through the fence using a feed bag, which is normally tied around a horse's neck at feeding time when it is out working in the fields.

On the third day, Joe wanted to know when I would go into the corral. By now, Sweetheart nuzzled me every time I approached the fence and was eating oats out of my hand. I told him I would enter the corral the next day but did not want him nearby. Joe was concerned that he would not be close enough to intervene if things went wrong. He said that he would have his gun ready if there was any possibility of me being trampled. "If you cannot tame her, I might as well get rid of her."

He also wanted me to have a lasso and a blacksnake—a short handle whip with a ten-foot lash. I refused. "All I need is a bucket of water and a sack of oats."

"Okay, it's your funeral," he said.

I did not feed or water Sweetheart that day. The next morning, I opened the gate just enough to get into the corral. By then I was sure that Sweetheart had accepted the human who spoke to her in a gentle voice. She stayed at the other end until I said something encouraging and then she slowly came toward me, no longer pawing and showing her teeth.

I placed the pail of water down and backed away. She walked slowly to the water, keeping a wary eye on me while I murmured sweet nothings. She smelt the pail, looked up, then lowered her head and started to drink.

Raising her head, she noticed the familiar feed bag. I emptied half on the ground, and stepped back three paces, keeping up with my mumble-jumble. My mind was active, not with fear but with where to put my hands on the top rail of the fence should I need to jump over. I need not have worried. Sweetheart finished and nuzzled me for the rest of the oats. I stayed in the corral for ten more minutes. Then, turning my back, I walked to the gate and let myself out.

Joe was upset because I had not touched Sweetheart, but his wife sensed what I was trying to do and reminded him he had promised to give me the time

I needed, and besides, I had tamed five other draft horses during the short time I had been there.

Joe brought the matter up again that evening, and his wife and daughter joined in. I surely needed their support. The daughter mentioned Blacky, a stallion that I had tamed on another ranch. They had heard an exaggerated story, so I told them what really happened.

Blacky had suffered the same brutality as the mare, and I was near to being trampled the first time he threw me. As he raced around the enclosure, voices yelled at me to get out. I had other ideas, because by then, a week had gone by and I sensed that Blacky would not harm me. After kicking up his heels for a few minutes, he stopped and looked over. Finally, he came close and poked me with his nose. When I thought it was time to move, I slowly rose to my feet.

Although he threw me a few more times, he always came and nuzzled me while I was lying there.

A week later, I was riding him bareback without a bridle. Man and horse became a team. I finished the story: "The only thing I put on his head was a halter with a short rope. I kept it short, because I did not want the rope to get tangled in his front legs and bring him down if I was unseated and he ran free."

Joe was finally convinced, and I took my time taming Sweetheart.

I LEFT THE RANCH in late November to work for Joe's brother who had a logging operation in Coleman, a small town in the Crow's Nest Pass in the Canadian Rockies, not far from the British Columbia border. Besides logging, the main industry was mining. Europeans worked in logging and English and Welsh worked in the mines. I may have been English, but I did not like work below ground, so I tried to find jobs where I could see the sun and clouds.

Joe's brother was happy to have someone who knew about horses, and I was hired as a teamster. The operation was small, with one skidder and one loader who operated the big machines, two cant hookers who wrestled the logs with their big hooks, one swamper who kept the road cleared, six sawyers who used different saws depending on what they were cutting, and two teamsters, including myself. The rest were bosses, loggers, and kitchen staff. In all, it was a thirty-man operation.

The sawyers cut the trees that had been blazed, or marked, by the timber boss. A log had to be at least ten inches in diameter at the smallest end, and some trees produced as many as three logs. The rest of the log was cut into four-foot lengths and used as cordwood.

We worked hard from sunup to sundown. A law required daylight work for safety reasons, but this did not prevent some operators from getting the loggers on the trail before daylight. In a larger camp, where I later worked, we had to plod several miles in the dark to reach the cutting area. This operation took its employees to the worksite on the log sleighs.

I drove a team of four horses hitched to a sleigh and took logs from the cutting area back to the sawmill. On steep, snowy hills, the loaded sleigh could potentially override the horses, but there was a safeguard: a box of sand that I could open by pulling a lever so the sand would be spread under the runners. Sparks would fly but the sleigh would slow down. Going up steep hills presented another problem; the horses would have trouble keeping their footing, even though they were shod to prevent slipping.

I worked without serious incident until the first week of March when a Chinook blew through. The first time I experienced a Chinook was in the foothills of the Rockies. I had remarked to someone that a rainstorm was heading our way.

He corrected me and explained that a black cloud was the sign of a warm wind blowing through the Crowsnest Pass. It was called a "Chinook," and if it lasted two or more days, it would melt the snow. Ranchers were happy, because their animals would not have to paw into the snow for their feed. Loggers, though, were not.

This Chinook had lasted two days, but it was well below freezing the day of the incident. I was on a trail, bringing in a load of logs, and had to use a frozen stream for about three hundred yards. In those days, a worker did not have safety laws to protect him when the boss insisted he do something unsafe. He knew that, if he refused, he would be fired, and the company would have no trouble finding someone else to do his job.

After talking with the boss (who was not a bad sort) about the danger of the load breaking through the ice, I agreed to drive the horses. When I reached the frozen stream, I stopped and went to each horse and talked to it while brushing the ice off its mouth and nostrils. Ice had built up because of their breathing. After checking the chains that bound the logs, I walked the dangerous stretch. I did not like what I found.

Returning to the team, I spoke quietly and held them with a tight rein as we advanced along the frozen stream. Just when I thought we had made it, the sleigh went through the ice and settled a couple of feet to the bottom. The horses pulled mightily but all they did was break more ice around them. When I managed to get them to stand still, I unhooked them from the sleigh, and they trotted off down the trail, leaving me there.

Freezing water had leaked into my boots, and my mitts were so stiff with ice that I could not remove them. Ice on my clothing made it difficult to move. I was cold and shivering, and my hands and feet were giving me a lot of pain.

I decided to take an overland route. It would be one mile instead of the three miles along the road. I struggled along in two feet of snow and my feet and hands became numb. More than once, I just wanted to lie down but knew I had to keep moving to have any chance of surviving.

I also knew that, when the horses reached camp, some of the loggers would be sent to look for me, and it would be easy to follow my trail through the trees. When the search party finally found me, I was still staggering along. I was helped back to the camp, where my hands and feet were soaked in cold water until the gloves and boots could be removed. I was then taken to the small hospital in Coleman.

My feet and hands thawed and began to hurt. On the third day, the skin peeled off, leaving them raw. I spent two months there while soft, new skin grew. The Workmen's Compensation Board paid my hospital bill and fifteen dollars for the first month after I was discharged. I was then considered able to do light work. (Like hell I was.)

I returned to the camp, where I worked for a few weeks by helping the cook as best I could. As soon as I was able to get moving again, I headed out. The logging season was over, and I decided to try my luck in Vancouver.

Chapter 4
WE WANT WORK WITH WAGES

I CONTINUED TO PICK up occasional jobs, but as the Depression deepened, things only got worse. By the spring of 1933, I was in Saskatoon and pretty near broke when I was hired as a carpenter, along with twenty others, to help build the Dundurn Relief Camp, some forty miles south of the city.

Relief camps were first set up by provincial governments in places like exhibition grounds. Many men were forced to go to the camps, because families were told their welfare would be reduced if a single unemployed man was living with them. These men could not live at home, there were no jobs, and they did not qualify for welfare. There was no way out. They were forced to become vagrants and considered a blight.

By early 1933, the camps had been transferred to federal jurisdiction and placed under military command with the Department of National Defence (DND). The DND built new camps in isolated areas as a means to confine and control the single unemployed, who were (it was thought) ripe for revolution. They were being taken out of towns and cities and swept under the rug.[5]

When I got to the Dundurn site, there was only one set of blueprints for the bunkhouses we were to build.[6] I soon learnt that not one of our bosses could read the simple blueprints, which rankled me because they were paid a salary of two hundred dollars a month, plus room, clothing, and food. We received two dollars a day (twelve dollars for a six-day week), out of which we paid five dollars "room and board," leaving us with seven dollars for the week. That was twenty-eight dollars a month compared to the bosses' two hundred dollars.

It took us three weeks to build eight bunkhouses with ten two-tier bunks on either side so they could house forty men. The two rows of bunks were eight feet apart, and there was a potbellied stove at each end, along with card tables. Each had a two-holer outhouse.[7]

When the work ended, I stayed on as an inmate on relief of $1.40 a week. We also received clothes and board and were given tobacco and cigarette papers. In our free time, we played card games, such as bridge or penny-ante poker, and took turns with chores like tending the stoves and sweeping and washing the floors.

There were now hundreds of us housed at the camp, sent by relief officers from the towns and cities. This included someone in each bunkhouse to inform on any who made trouble. My trouble-making reputation began when my buddies suggested that draft deflectors be attached to the windows to prevent cold air from pouring in on the lower bunks. I was chosen to present the request, but before I could talk directly with the commander of the camp, I had to go through three administrators. I even had to present a blueprint before this simple job was finally allowed. This would seem to be a reasonable request, but I was now considered a troublemaker.

It was the "work" we were ordered to do that really got under my skin: digging a seven-foot-deep ditch, forty-feet long, over two days, and filling it in the next. When I had opted to stay on at the camp, I was assured we would have useful work. I could not find any use in digging a hole and filling it in again. It was not long before I left to try my luck elsewhere.[8]

The next couple of years were ones of bare survival. When I got desperate, I stayed in relief camps but would end up being kicked out for "agitating." By May 1935, I was in a British Columbia camp, where I spent two weeks before being discovered. I was escorted out by two RCMP officers—Royal Canadian Mounted Police—who told me I was on a list of those not to be admitted into any federal government camps. I had suspected this and wondered why it took so long for that BC camp commander to find out I was there. I do admit that I moved my three given names around to avoid detection, but I never changed my surname.

I headed to Vancouver, and a short while later, there was a strike in the relief camps to protest the militaristic and hopeless conditions. Prime Minister R. B. Bennett had led the conservative government for those first five years of the Depression, and we held him responsible for our miserable state.

Men left the camps and began arriving in Vancouver, where we held demonstrations. That was when the idea for the On-To-Ottawa Trek took hold. After careful planning by our leaders, we hopped the CPR freights as a group and headed to Ottawa, intending to present our complaints personally to R. B. Bennett.

Just before the trek started on June 4, 1935, I met one of the leaders, James "Red" Walsh, a Communist Party of Canada member who was with the Relief Camp Worker's Union. Red's nickname did not necessarily reflect his political affiliation; with his red hair and ruddy complexion, "Red" suited him to a tee. He was a good organizer, and though our contacts were brief, I developed a deep respect for him.

Before leaving Vancouver, the route was established, advance committees set up, and stops planned for each night. The advance committees arranged for food donations and places to billet the boys, such as exhibition grounds. Community committees set up soup kitchens, arranged for clothing donations, and organized tag days to raise money.

A few of us were chosen to make sure our group conducted itself in the best way possible. We impressed this upon those who joined us at stops along the way and got rid of any trouble makers, often undercover police. This discipline was critical to ensure the support of the townspeople along the way.

Among other stops, there was a three-day stay in Calgary and one day each in Medicine Hat and Moose Jaw. Wives and girlfriends wanted to join the trek in Calgary, but this was deemed problematic so arrangements were made for them to travel with the advance group.

More joined us along the route with many on top of the freights or hanging off the sides. We held marches in the towns and cities, holding signs that demanded an end to the "Slave Camps," or read, "We Want Work With Wages." Each group of forty trekkers had a parade marshal. We also had men who surrounded the speakers' platform to ensure police infiltrators did not cause trouble.

Red Walsh, and other leaders, kept our morale up with speeches, which also convinced the citizens that our trip to Ottawa would benefit all Canadians; they were just as frustrated with their own conditions as we trekkers were with ours. News media gave us favourable coverage and mentioned how well-disciplined we were, even during our stay in Regina where things were about to change and not because of us.

It turned out the federal government wanted everything possible done to bring the trek to an end in Regina. The trek committee knew that the government was sending the RCMP to Regina. Even the City of Regina police had orders to stop us. They planned to arrest our leaders, hoping that the majority of us would disband.

July 1, 1935, Dominion Day, was the day that those in power called the "Regina Riot." We called it "the use of force to halt the trek." Part of the government's strategy had been to bring three of our committee members to Ottawa where they presented our requests for fair wages and meaningful work, but the meeting ended in a shouting match when the government representatives started calling us a bunch of bums and Reds.

In the meantime, in Regina, we arranged a public meeting, just as we had at every stop along the way. The speakers' platform would be well-guarded by boys who could be trusted. We used a borrowed rope to keep anyone unknown to us away from the platform. The speakers were two of our leaders and a local minister.

Only about two hundred trekkers were at the meeting that evening. Most others were concerned citizens, including women and children. One of our leaders started to tell the crowd about what had happened in Ottawa. At that point, I was facing away from the speaker and making small talk with a mother who had a baby in a carriage.

Then ... mayhem.

There was a blast from a whistle, and suddenly, police were everywhere, mounted and on foot, swinging clubs at any person in their way. It was violent and inhumane. Before I could sort out what was happening, a policeman's horse knocked over the carriage with the baby in it, and the mother was covering her child with her body to protect it from the horse's hooves.

Somebody gripped one of the horse's reins, and it reared. At the same time, I pulled on the policeman's leg and he struck at me with his club, missing my head and glancing off my shoulder. The policeman was unseated and somebody else pulled at the strap around his wrist in an attempt to remove his club, while he defended himself from people trying to strike him in the face with their fists.

I saw this out of the corner of my eye as I helped to get the mother and baby to safety. I received a blow at this point and woke up in a jail cell with two others, one who lived in Regina, the other a union member. I was released the next morning after a Justice of the Peace decided that attending a public meeting was not a crime.

I stayed in Regina long enough to read accounts of what happened. It was confirmed that a policeman had been killed and many injured on both sides. Our hopes for some kind of government action to lift us from our despair were dashed. There was nothing for me to do except slip back into my wandering life. With no jobs, I had no choice but to stay in relief camps, or as we called them, "slave camps."

By November 1935, I was back at Dundurn, the camp I had helped build two years before. This time I was to last six weeks before being escorted out. The top man had been a major in the First World War. He was assisted by two officers from the same war. And just like the army, a bugler woke us up early and signaled lights out at night.

A third of the camp's inmates were so-called administrators. They had an officers' mess with their own cooks. When food was delivered, their cooks would confiscate the best vegetables and cuts of meat. Some of the single unemployed held office positions because of their skills in shorthand and typing. Others were assigned to chores such as cleaning, tending the wood stoves, and shining the officers' boots. The rest of us were in the barracks—the rank-and-filers.

This time around, I spent five weeks as a member of an inmate's committee. We had held three mild demonstrations, each of which ended with some kind of concession from the brass. Of course, this meant I was on the blacklist, but I had yet to be kicked out.[9]

The others who behaved themselves were given passes to show to a uniformed soldier before being allowed to leave the ten-acre compound, now enclosed by a six-foot wire fence topped with three strands of barbed wire. I wanted to get out with the others, so we devised a plan. One of the guys would exit the compound, go along the outside to a spot where we would not be observed, and hand me his pass through the fence.

The reasons for getting out were to be found in a small village about five miles away. We would make a beeline to the pub for a pint or so of beer, which cost five cents each. We also visited the drugstore, which must have made a fortune in selling the rubbing alcohol we used for spiking our beer. Another attraction was the girls; we gave them a dollar for ten minutes in a rented room. That is what they existed on. The drugstore had "under-the-counter" aids regarding these activities.

When we arrived back at the camp, the plan was that somebody would distract the gate keeper while I slipped through. The second time I tried this trick, I was found out and taken to the office where I was told that if I broke the rules again, I would be kicked out.

When I left the office, one of the men who had a job in administration told me that the reason I was not discharged immediately was because the Rigg Commission was due to arrive the next day and the top brass did not want any disturbances. Some of us already knew that a Federal Government commission, headed by someone named Rigg, was to visit the camp at some point to find out why there was so much unrest in these wonderful places that had been built all across Canada.[10, 11, 12]

When I went back to barracks, I told my buddies of the imminent arrival of the Rigg Commission. Our small protest group held a meeting and put together a list of requests to present.[13] It was then typed by one of our members. We read the list to the men, and over 95 percent signed a petition for representatives of the inmates to meet with the Commission.

Later that night, we received word from our contact in the administration office to expect good meals during the commissioners' visit. He also told us that the top brass had chosen their own four-man committee to represent the inmates. That was the straw that broke the camel's back.

The men blew their tops, and decided they would refuse to go out with the picks and shovels the next day. We agreed that the kitchen staff would go to work, along with those providing other essential services.

Next morning, we ate the best breakfast we had ever had at the camp. Normally, it was burnt toast, rubbery eggs, leathery pancakes, and half-cooked oatmeal porridge with chewy lumps. This time the food had been well-prepared, because two of the administration's cooks had supervised our kitchen staff.

After breakfast, we pitched in to clean the huts because we knew that nobody would be assigned to work that morning, for the simple reason that the men were not going to answer the roll call. The bugle sounded but not one man responded.

The brass was notified and supervisors were sent to the bunkhouses, demanding that we line up for roll call so we could be assigned to work. They wanted things to run smoothly for the visit of the Rigg Commission. The mildest reply was, "Go to hell!" We made it clear we were not going out to work until our own men, not the major's, could present our grievances. We knew we had the administration on the spot and won our right to meet with the Commission. Some of the men then picked up their shovels and played a game of digging, but most were chewing the fat and playing cards or board games.

At eleven-thirty, the bugle signaled us to wash up for the midday meal. We had seen the menu posted on the bulletin board the day before. It was to be buffalo meat. We had had buffalo the previous week, and though tasty, it was so tough that one of the men nailed his portion to his boot. He was forced to remove it after four days because of the smell.

We decided to present a piece of that day's buffalo to the Commission as proof of its inedible condition. We were fooled! This time the brass sent their own cooks to the inmates' cook house. The meal was wonderful. Of course, it was eaten by the Commission members too, to show how well fed we were.

It was three o'clock when the inmate delegation was given orders to go to the administration building. There, we met with the three members of the Rigg Commission. I had been chosen to present our requests.[14]

The first issue had to do with the degrading conditions in the camp and the fact that we were under military rule. It was quite a heated discussion. Our second point was that the camp was supposed to give us work of a useful nature. This did not mean digging trenches one day and filling them in the next. By now, the meeting was turning into a free-for-all and the chair adjourned the meeting until nine o'clock the next morning.

I had tried to stay calm during the meeting, but that night we received so much advice that, after a little encouragement (that I did not need), I agreed to call a spade a spade, to change our requests to demands, and to threaten a demonstration if the conditions were not met.

The next morning, we got to the food issue. I told the commissioners how the bosses' cooks had the first choice of meat, vegetables, and canned goods and how the food was good when it was sent to our cook house, but lousy when it was served, even canned food. I then talked about graft; how when unloading trucks, I had seen meat, canned goods, and even tools, all meant for us, covered with sacks and taken out again, obviously destined for the camp overseers.

The meeting was somewhat stormy because the major denied all charges, telling the committee members we were a bunch of trouble makers. Three days later, two of our committee had left the camp voluntarily and three had been discharged. I was the only one left.[15]

That night, the outside toilets were destroyed, and a fire was started in one of the buildings. The next day, I was accused of being involved. Though I had little to do with those incidents, I did know something about breaking into the toolshed and burying the picks and shovels in a trench.

The next afternoon, I was ordered to report to the office. There I was met by the major who charged me with destroying government property. Two RCMP officers escorted me to my bunkhouse to pack my belongings. Within twenty minutes, I was being driven out of the camp.

Chapter 5
BROUGHT TO OUR KNEES

WHILE THE YOUNGER MAN drove, the older grey-haired officer sat with me in the rear. He said that they were not taking me to jail as there was no evidence that would stand up in court. Besides, he thought that if I was put in the witness box the newspapers would have a field day with the government's treatment of the single unemployed.

An hour went by, and it was starting to rain. I pinned him down, asking where was I going. He said that they had orders to drop me in an isolated spot. They soon stopped, wished me luck, and each gave me a dollar, a lot of money. One of them rummaged around in the trunk and gave me a raincoat. I signed a receipt for the money and raincoat, and they drove away.[16] [17]

I looked around. It was dusk, and there was nothing in sight except their rear lights disappearing in the distance. The raincoat did not have a hood, so I put it over my head to try to keep my neck and packsack dry. The mud on the road was ankle deep, and it was not long before I was soaked to the skin and my boots were full of mud and water. Hours went by. If only I could find a straw stack to burrow into until morning. At one point, I thought I saw one, only to find a pile of rocks. I was tired and downhearted.

Suddenly, I noticed a light. I lit a cigarette and checked my cheap Ingersoll watch. It was ten-thirty. By now I was hungry enough to enjoy one of the lousy camp meals. I climbed a wire fence and headed directly for the light, only to find I was in a plowed field with my boots being sucked into the mud with every step. To console myself, I hoped the part I played with the Rigg Commission would benefit the men confined in the camp.

While I was musing, I came to a pasture, crossed to the house, and knocked on the door. It was opened by a man who invited me to enter. I mentioned that I would dirty the kitchen floor, and heard a woman's voice telling me to wait a moment while she laid out some newspapers.

I took my boots off and placed them on the porch before entering the house. As I sat on the chair they offered, a strange feeling overcame me. So many times when I knocked on a farmer's door, offering to work in exchange for a meal and a place to sleep, there would be questions. What was my name? Where was I from? Where was I going? This time there were none.

As I was thinking, I heard the couple talking and addressing each other as "Mary" and "Frank." Frank gave me a cup of coffee laced with a little rye whiskey. "Here, this will warm you up."

He put a copper container on the stove to heat water for a bath and got some dry clothes to replace the muddy outfit I was wearing. Meanwhile, his wife was cooking bacon, eggs, and potatoes. During the meal, I told them about the RCMP officers leaving me on a muddy road and of the light that attracted me when I sorely needed it. It was now well after eleven o'clock—late for a farmer.

That night, after my bath, I slept in their son's room. I woke the next morning to find the sun shining. I owed my new friends something to repay their kindness, but when I said I was ready to split some wood before I moved on, they said they hoped I would stay awhile, and not address them as Mr. and Mrs. The rest of my stay I called Mary "Mum" and her husband "Frank."

During the time I remained with these good people, we talked a lot about the Depression, and they told me that their son had left home to find a job. At first, they had received a letter every week, the last sent from Vancouver with no return address. They were concerned because they had not heard from him for several weeks and were leaving the light in the window, hoping for his return. I promised I would look out for him, since I was going to Vancouver next, but I never did come across him.

Mary and Frank's situation was typical. Their crops were gone because of drought, and they could not even get loans for seed, so the sons struck out on their own. Their parents had only enough to support themselves and their daughters.

I stayed there for that wonderful time, helping Frank build a barbed-wire fence. This was no easy task. It was a mile long and each post—they were twenty feet apart—had to have a hole made using a manual auger. The fence was to protect Frank's meagre crop by keeping the cattle out.

Frank and Mary's light beckoned me after three-and-a-half long years of hardscrabble existence in the middle of the Depression. I will always remember Mary's words after I had been welcomed into that home: "Frank, I knew the lamp in the window would attract somebody who needed help on a night like this."

I had travelled thousands of miles, from Montreal to Vancouver, and met many caught up in the despair of the "Dirty Thirties." My goal, like theirs, was to survive. I tried my hand at any job you could name, including sign painting for lodges and cottagers at Lake of the Woods in northwestern Ontario, but it was always short-lived. Jobs were so scarce that, to get one, you often had to pay the foreman part of your wage.

People without jobs were classed as vagrants by politicians and by anyone who wore a uniform or badge. Thousands of us were given the bum's rush out of town more than once. I was in a prison cell three times, once after the Regina Riot, and twice on charges of being a vagrant: "a person without means of support."

I look back with amusement at one of those times. Three of us found ourselves stranded in a small town after a couple of railway bulls kicked us off a boxcar. Bulls regularly pushed us off the trains, even at forty miles an hour. Hands could be smashed and limbs broken. It was late at night as we hunted for a place to bed down. One of the boys told us he had an uncle on the outskirts of town.

At some point, when riding the rails, Jim Higgins hopped off a freight train at Lake of the Woods in Northwestern Ontario, near the Manitoba border, where he found a few jobs chopping wood and painting signs for cottagers and resort owners.

The first barn we came to just happened to be his "uncle's." Despite my misgivings, I climbed up to the loft, and settled down in the hay. The next morning, we were rudely awakened by his supposed uncle holding a shotgun.

He marched us to his entrance gate where a cop was waiting to take us to the town lockup. By noon, we had been let go by the Justice of the Peace with orders to leave town and not return. He told us the owner had changed his mind on the trespassing charge.

My two companions headed for the railroad to keep on moving, but I went back to the farmhouse to tell the folks I was sorry for trespassing. I thought it was probably a stupid thing to do, but once I make up my mind, hell and high water cannot deter me. I chuckle when I think back on what happened next.

I opened the gate and was greeted by a friendly dog—clearly not a watch-dog. I had run across many of those. The man who opened the door also appeared friendly. When I apologized, and told him I appreciated that he had dropped the trespassing charge, he laughed and invited me in to share the meal I had interrupted.

I learnt that he had gone through three crop failures because of drought, and that the bank owned the farm because of unpaid loans. He and his family had been allowed to stay until it was sold and were able to keep a car, two horses, and some chickens. He also had a windmill. He had borrowed money to pay the drillers when they had to go down over three hundred feet to find water, but the bank could not repossess the windmill. The water it pumped was enough for his three-acre garden, which provided plenty of food for the family.

He was also better off than many of his friends because he lived within the town limits. The town gave him employment, such as garbage collection, and he helped with fires. In the winter, he plowed the sidewalks. All this meant that he was in the fortunate position of not having to abandon his farm. Hundreds of others were forced to leave everything behind and look for greener pastures where none could be found.

Hundreds of thousands were feeling the devastating effects of what we now know as "the Great Depression," but 1935 was the year that brought even the most stubborn to their knees. Yet it continued. Relentlessly. I was a good listener and avid reader, and though I knew I could not believe everything I read, I did know what was happening to the common people.

I also felt I knew what was going on politically in the rest of the world. The so-called socialist parties had their own brand of party line. The same thing was happening in what were considered democratic forms of government. Hitler had Nazi Germany under his control and those who opposed him were being rounded up. Mussolini had been the fascist premier of Italy since 1922, and had slowly been putting his country on a war footing. The League of Nations, established in 1920 to promote peace, had shown it did not have the power to do its job.

By the fall of 1937, two depressing years after seeing that welcome light in the window, I was in Saskatoon and thinking of volunteering to fight in the Spanish Civil War. It had started a year earlier, and the democratically elected government of Spain needed help in its fight against the rebel forces of General Franco and his allies, Hitler and Mussolini.

While I could not fully commit myself to any political organization, I did associate with many causes that I thought were worthy, such as workers' rights and trying to improve the lot of the single unemployed. This seemed like a worthy cause, if ever there was one.

I knew the Communist Party was involved, and had even been asked many times to become an official member, but resisted because I did not want to be tied down, to become a robot. I wanted to be independent and decide myself if a cause was worth fighting for.

I was coming out of a Saskatoon Labour Council meeting when someone asked, "How about going over there, Jim?" That was when I made the decision. I paid part of my passage, and some came from the unions. The rest came from the local Ukrainian and Polish organizations.[18]

I signed on as an anti-fascist to fight in the Spanish Civil War. Defending democracy was a cause worth fighting for—one I could fully commit to.

Portrait of Jim Higgins taken in Saskatoon before he left to fight in the Spanish Civil War—possibly his passport photo.

Chapter 6
OVER THE PYRENEES[19]

I HAD TO GET into Spain illegally because, earlier in 1937, Canada passed its Foreign Enlistment Act meant to keep Canadians from volunteering to fight in Spain.[20] [21] By now, it was October. To throw the authorities off my scent, I went to London first. As a British subject, I did not need a passport to get there.

I used my Canadian passport to get into France and arrived in Paris with five others on the same mission, an Englishman from Liverpool and four others from Canada, all immigrants like myself.[22] You might say that we Canadians represented five countries besides Canada: Italy, Finland, Sweden, France, and England. All spoke passable English, but even the Liverpool man and myself had a bit of trouble communicating because of our accents. However, with a little sign language, we were able to understand each other.

We had come to Paris to enlist as volunteers, to fight with the Spanish people against General Franco, who was supported by Hitler and Mussolini in his 1936 military coup against Spain's democratically elected government. No country in Europe or the West came to the aid of the Spanish government.[23] A year later, there would be only myself and the French-Canadian left alive.

The French-Canadian helped us find the Paris recruiting centre, where we were checked for security clearance before being transported to the Spanish border. Not everyone who tried to enlist was taken. We were each questioned about our activities during the three previous years. Those accepted had been active in trade unions and political parties that were trying to alleviate the oppression of the poor during the depression. Mercenaries were rejected.[24]

I passed with no trouble since I had proof of my activities, including letters from three organizations in Canada. None were from the Communist Party. I was required to turn over all personal belongings, except my passport, and was given a letter highly recommending me as a volunteer. I was to give the letter to the commander where I would spend my first four days in Spain.

Within two days of enlisting, I left on a bus to the Spanish border with twenty other volunteers. I was to make them understand that drinking on the bus would endanger the whole operation, and also to make sure that letters some of us had received from the recruiting centre were destroyed if we were arrested by the French police. I was introduced, by first name only, to two others who had the same orders. "Carl" could speak five languages and "Rene" was strong in English and French and could understand German.

We kept off the main road and our ride south was uninterrupted. About seventy kilometers from Perpignan, a French village at the foot of the Pyrenees Mountains, we transferred to another bus and driver. We were now on a country road away from any villages.

By this time, it was known that Carl, Rene, and I were responsible for the safety and conduct of the volunteers. Carl and Rene told me that, when we reached Perpignan, they would be returning to Paris and that a guide would contact me before the climb started.

Carl had noticed a man named Rick asking too many questions and told me to let the others know they should string him along but not tell him their surnames, country of origin, or who aided them to get to Paris.

Before we changed buses that afternoon, we were advised to get some sleep along the side of the road. We were going over the Pyrenees that night and would need all the energy we could muster.[25]

While we dozed, an incident occurred that illustrated the need for security. Carl and Rene invited me to go with them while they asked Rick a few questions away from the group. There was no malice in Carl's voice when he asked, "Who are you, and why are you with these volunteers?"

Rick admitted he had no plans to go to Spain but was concerned about the people in Paris who had been taken in by his ruse to travel with the volunteers.

It turned out he was a reporter for an English paper using a false name and fake papers.

He said, "I didn't get much information; I found the men very close-mouthed when I asked any questions. I just wish I had the guts to go with them into Spain. If I do write anything, I will stress that I found them sincere and dedicated to a cause."

Carl and Rene went out of hearing to discuss the problem. When they returned, they told Rick they accepted his story and would allow him to continue on to Perpignan. He was to return with them to Paris, so that a check could be made with the newspaper. Carl asked me not to mention our conversation to anyone else on the bus. I was to sit with Rick and be friendly so the others would not know about our discussion.

"Now," Carl said, "get some rest, because you will need it." I had not slept for eighteen hours so had no problem dozing off.

I was awakened by Rene shaking my shoulder. "We'll be leaving in ten minutes," he told me, "but first, here's what to expect." He told me the bus was equipped with a two-way radio that was in a box under the driver's seat. It kept us in contact with two cars for security, one a mile ahead and one a mile behind.

He also mentioned that food and skins of weak wine would be taken aboard the bus after leaving Perpignan, and that we would receive instructions after we left the bus a little further on. "There might be a problem unless everyone realizes the importance of letting the driver and me do the talking at the roadblock in Perpignan."

When we boarded the bus, I joked with Rick and took him to the rear. While the rest were singing songs, I got a lesson in how the news media used trickery to get a story. Although I knew this went on, it was the first time I was given details.

Rick told me that an ace reporter had been sent two months before, but he had stood out like a tree in the desert. He was exposed by an English volunteer before he even left Paris and was told not to try the stunt again. So, this time, the newspaper had chosen someone who was not well known.

We arrived in Perpignan at dusk and were stopped by three French guards on a narrow, cobbled street. Carl, Rene, and the driver got out while we sang songs in different languages. During the journey, Carl told me that this was not the first time he had taken a group to the border and let me know what to expect, unless the guards had been changed since his last trip.

We had been lucky; the guard in charge was the same, and I was not surprised when they shook hands like old comrades. Within ten minutes, our men got back on the bus and we drove towards the foot of the Pyrenees. It was dark by the time we reached a spot where the bus could go no further. A car was waiting for Carl and Rene, and they headed back to Paris with Rick.

We were on our own.

All joking ceased as we realized what was confronting us. I was ready to adjust to anything, and it struck me that life as I had known it was forever in the past. We sat on the ground in a wide-open cave where we were given rope-soled shoes, called *alpargatas*, and hung our own shoes around our necks.

Our guide was a rugged Spaniard named José. He spoke quietly and told us, in good English, what lay ahead that night. He introduced a man named "Bill" and said, "I will lead, and Bill will be in the rear. There is to be no smoking, because there is a French border post near here and smoke hangs in the air for a long time. This route is fairly safe because the no-smoking order has been obeyed."

He emphasized that it was extremely important not to alert the border guards with smoke or anything else. "You noticed that the bus was driven with no lights during the last three miles?" I had noticed, and at times wondered how the driver managed to stay on the twisting road without going over a cliff. I learnt later that he had done the route so often that he could have driven it "with his eyes shut."

"Noise is another problem—this is why you are wearing the *alpargatas*— and I would request that you not talk any more than you have to." He acknowledged that noise could not be entirely contained, but since the border guards did not patrol at night, we had less chance of trouble. While he was talking, we received sausage and bread, along with wine. This was to be the last time we ate on French soil.

José looked at his watch and said, "Let's go; unless we have trouble, we will be in Spain by daybreak." The first half hour was easy going on a well-worn smugglers' trail. We kept in single file, about six feet apart. I wondered when we were going to start climbing, because it seemed as though we were going down as much as we were going up. It was only later that I realized we had been going up more than down.

After we were beyond any danger of the border guards hearing us, and while it was still relatively easy going, I chatted quietly with José. I learnt there were numerous paths across the mountains, and that many of the guides were professional smugglers, each with his own route, some of which mules could travel on partway. Often, it was a family business and sometimes two families were involved, one on each side of the border.

The smugglers lived in isolated villages at the foot of the Pyrenees, and often the whole village depended on smuggling. They were closely knit and communicated in a bastard language, a mix of French and Spanish. Some of these villages consisted of only five or six families, while others could have up to a hundred.

Later in the war, I learnt from one of these mountain people, who surprised me with his knowledge of English, that each village had its own school, and even the children in hamlets were taught the three Rs in the evenings. I found that these people could be trusted and were, in their own way, aiding the elected government.

José and I stopped chatting as we left the path, and the real climb—I should say nightmare—began. There was no moon, the air was crisp and calm, and the stars were the brightest I had ever seen. We were lucky in that respect.

We had left non-essentials behind so were not burdened down. Most of us kept only cigarettes and tobacco. I had about twenty packs of cigarettes in a small packsack that I had brought with me from Canada. Besides myself, only José and Bill had packsacks but theirs held food and first-aid equipment.

In single file, close enough to touch the person ahead, we struggled on and came upon our first big obstacle—a forty-foot ledge, about four feet wide in some places and less than two feet in others. If it had been flat, it would not have been much of a problem, but it was uneven, sometimes slippery, and sloped in places toward the edge.

José tied a rope to a stunted tree, carefully made his way across holding onto it, and hitched the other end around a bush where the ledge broadened out to a flat area with a rock overhang. With Bill's help, we each squeezed behind the rope and inched our way across with our backs against the face of the cliff. I made the crossing without incident but was scared as hell.

One of the boys gave us something to think about when he froze halfway across. José took care of it by going out to where he was, quietly assuring him while holding his arm, and guiding him the rest of the way. I felt somewhat safer because the rope-soled shoes seemed to give a better hold. They were the same kind I was to wear much of my time in Spain.

After that, we had it fairly easy, going up and sometimes down, until the rocky surface became damp and treacherous and the climb got harder. At times we helped each other scale six-to-eight-foot rock faces to get to another ledge. Somebody sprained an ankle, and we took turns helping him. We came to a fast-flowing mountain stream and used the rope to pull our way across. By this time, we were wet and cold. Slight injuries and a couple of new ankle cases were reported.

Hours had gone by, and I wondered if we would ever get to the top. We had rested briefly about six times, but even so, the thin atmosphere, coupled with snow between the rocks, was getting to us. I was stumbling, and through bleary eyes, could see that others were in a state of exhaustion. José was carrying somebody who had sprained an ankle; he had tried to make it without help and had passed out. I realized then how tough and strong our guide was.

While I was questioning if I could make it much further, José called a halt and led us into a large cave. He laid the injured man down and Bill came in, helping two others who had been hurt. Although we were told we could smoke, no one did. A smoke was the last thing I wanted. I felt as though I could sleep the rest of my life.

After we settled down, José and Bill opened their packs and brought out food and some large well-protected bottles. They poured some of the contents into tin cups and gave us the drink with a hunk of cheese and bread.

By the time the drink reached me, I could see many of the others coming to life and really going to town on their bread and cheese. I asked Bill what it was and he answered, "a very good brandy." I swallowed and felt it burning. A glow took over my whole body, and I too came alive, ate my rations, and had a smoke.

José said we had made good time; that it had taken just eight-and-a-half hours to reach this point—eight-and-a-half hours of pure hell as far as I was concerned. "You are now in Spain and can rest a bit." I asked what time it was; my own timepiece had stopped, because it had been dunked when I slipped crossing a stream. Bill, who was resting beside me, said it was five a.m.

A bit later, with the others dead to the world, he asked me why I was not sleeping. I told him my thoughts were keeping me awake. We had another shot of brandy and started to talk. He told me he was from England and that he was a graduate of Oxford. His parents were pretty well-fixed. His activities included football, boxing, and swimming.[26]

Bill was the black sheep of his family, since he wrote for periodicals of the left, a "no-no" as far as they were concerned. When he volunteered in Paris, he was told they needed aids for the local guides, people who could communicate with the volunteers. He was a natural since he could climb, as well as make himself understood in four languages.

Over the two days that Bill and I talked, I discovered we had a lot in common, especially that we were both individualists. Neither of us was a card-carrying political member, but both of us were connected with movements on the left. We were trusted in the inner circles of certain parties and invited to their meetings.

I had always been secretive, but with Bill I felt I could ease up on information about myself. I had not been so trusting of anybody before. There were very few I would call a real friend. Bill felt like a friend.

This was to be Bill's last climb. It was tougher than his first, because it was already heading into winter in the mountains. He would stay with our group and go down into Spain. He had chosen this hard way to learn about the volunteers who went over the Pyrenees and planned to write about them, saying, "Only with experience can one write truthfully."

Through his observations, Bill had grown to recognize each man's skills. "For example," he said, "if you were in an ugly situation, would you want an individual by your side like the one who froze on the ledge?"

45

"No," I responded, "but I was really afraid myself, and it took all my will-power to make the crossing."

He went on to explain, "We all offer something different," and told me that the man who froze was an expert machinist. He could be as useful keeping the trucks running as anyone going to the front with a rifle. "Without people like him in the rear, transportation would come to a halt." I learnt later that the machinist was attached to a truck repair pool and did a damned good job.

We were roused by José, and within minutes, continued climbing in the dark. It was daybreak as we reached the top. I will never forget that moment when I gazed for the first time on Spain and the Mediterranean. The sight from the summit of the Pyrenees remains one of my cherished memories.

Nor shall I ever forget the last sight when I was leaving. A wealth of experience, of love and hate, passed between that first glimpse and the last. But for now, fascism and war seemed a long way off. Everything was so peaceful. The sea was calm, and the sun shone on its ripples, creating a dazzling array of glittering emeralds. I would have liked to savour the scene but Bill called out, "You going to stand there all day? The others are away ahead."

As I clambered down, I shouted, "Have you ever seen a view like that before?"

"No," he responded, "but I've seen it the other way, overcast and cloudy with an angry, raging sea. That's another sight to see." We caught up to the rest and reached a well-travelled mule path.

We wound our way down and came to a monastery where we were welcomed in Spanish by a monk. He led us to a large room filled with straw pallets, about two inches thick. Two monks worked at a huge stove and two others tended the injured. Stretchers and crutches were leaning against the wall.

We were given coffee and stew with bread. Then we stretched out on the pallets and rested until it was time to go down to where a truck was waiting to take us to an eighteenth-century stone fort at Figueres, the gathering spot for those of us who had arrived through France.[27] [28]

THOUSANDS OF VOLUNTEERS HAD come from around the world to support Spain's democracy. Fascism was on the rise and we all knew what was going on.

I had heard stories about Hitler's Germany from Jewish people who managed to get to Canada. It was not a secret. We all knew Hitler and Mussolini were supporting Franco, contravening the Non-Intervention Agreement they had signed, and that the Republican government did not have the army. Franco had the army. By the time I arrived, civilians in Guernica had been bombed, and the rebels had taken over half of Spain.[29]

There had been no central command on the Republican side at the beginning of the war. Unions and political factions had set up separate militias but were fighting an enemy unified under officers who were sons of the rich, with help from troops and modern weapons of war supplied by Hitler and Mussolini. It was only later, once the Republicans had time to organize an army, that full unity developed with the Spanish forces on the Republican side.

Most of us volunteers in the International Brigades, which were set up to assist the Republicans, came from labour or socialist backgrounds, but there were also a few intellectuals and writers. Some volunteers were outright communists and a few of those were made into generals right away. That was a big mistake, because they were no damn good as officers.

The odd volunteer thought he would go to Spain, have a bullet whiz by his head, and then go home, but he found out it was tough to get out after you enlisted. Most of us were good dedicated people. We were all anti-fascist, including the Germans and Italians who saw what was happening in their own countries. Nothing was broken down along ethnic or religious lines. One black guy told me, "This is the first time I've ever felt free. I feel so safe here." We were all together, with no difference of race, creed, or colour.

It ended up being language that determined things. At the beginning, when the internationals started arriving, all languages were jumbled together, but training proved impossible and they had to create battalions of soldiers who could understand each other. A few months before I arrived, the government forces sorted the English-speaking volunteers into five battalions under the 15th International Brigade.

Once Canadian volunteers got close to official battalion strength of twelve hundred, those who spoke and understood English were put into the

(*left*) Saul Wellman and Edward C. Smith

(*below*) Members of the machine-gun
company. Makela is second from right.

Lower image: *Mac-Pap Machine Gun Company, taken December 1937 at Mas de las Matas,
Teruel, Spain. Using a pen mark, Higgins identified himself as the man on the gun. Most,
though, were Finnish-Canadians. Niilo Makela, who became company commander, is standing second from the right. Within a few months, many would be killed in action or executed
by Franco's troops, including the highly respected Makela.* **Upper image:** *Saul Wellman,
Political Commissar to the Mac-Paps, and Edward Cecil-Smith, their Commander.*[30] [31]

Mackenzie-Papineau Battalion.[32] It was topped up with Americans and quite a few Spanish lads. Even so, I started out in an English company.

The Canadian battalion was named after William Lyon Mackenzie and Louis-Joséph Papineau, both of whom fought for political reform in Upper and Lower Canada in 1837-38. We referred to ourselves as Mac-Paps, and our commander was Edward Cecil-Smith, a Canadian journalist who later became a major.

WHILE WE WERE STILL at the fort, we were taught certain things with wooden rifles and how to jump out of a moving train when it was being bombed. Also, how to keep apart and not bunch up. Staying apart was important to reduce the size of the target.

We then went by train to Albacete, where the battalions were being trained. They found out I was a good shot with a rifle, and I was sent to a special camp for machine-gun training.[33] They taught us how to infiltrate the bullets by aiming just in front of the enemy's feet so they would have a body's length to hit as it was falling. It was important to keep the fire low, because the gun always went up a little when fired.

We learnt to conserve ammunition by firing single shots or a burst of five and were taught how to take the guns apart while blindfolded. The instructor would move the parts around, and still blindfolded, we would put them back together. I was pretty fast, and on November 30, 1937, I was transferred to special machine-gun duty.[34] [35] [36] [37] [38]

Chapter 7
AT ANY COST [39]

THE MAC-PAPS WERE AT rest, camped in an olive grove near the Aragon front when our commander, Major Edward Cecil-Smith, received word that the fascists had broken through the government's line. Franco's large-scale offensive to cut Republican Spain in two had begun.[40] It was the second week of March 1938, and by now, I had seen battle and been to Officer Training School.[41] [42]

The fascists attacked with overwhelming force and our battalion found itself in a hopeless situation with no orders except to "hold the lines." We knew we were sitting ducks. Later, I learnt the lines of communication had been broken. Six runners had been sent with orders to retire, but they never reached our commander. By the time the seventh runner made it through, we had gone through hell and lost many comrades.

These next two chapters describe what befell me during those few days.

TO ENSURE THERE WOULD be no delays when orders did arrive, we cleaned the guns, checked our ammo, and slept with our boots on. The next afternoon, two squads from the machine-gun company (my own included) were chosen to go point-to-point to find out from the outpost guards where the main body of fascists was concentrating. We were using a truck but were off it most of the time because bomber planes were playing tag with us. Fortunately, they went wide of the mark.

We returned with our report at nine p.m. and found our battalion beginning to move. At midnight, we passed through the ruined village of Azuara, which had been evacuated two days before. From then on, progress was very slow as we worked under the most difficult conditions on a very dark night.

Scouts went ahead and out to our flanks. Runners reporting back from the scouts were late and the battalion, unknowingly, went through enemy lines. The scouts at last managed to get messages through to advise us of the danger. We faced about and quietly slipped back. Meanwhile, the enemy had advanced under cover of night, knowing that no line was confronting them.

About one thirty a.m., the main body of the battalion was led to a wooded ravine with orders to rest until the command received the full report of the scouts. We would then have some idea of where our position should be when day broke.

I went to where I was to rest with my squad and fell over what I thought was another squad of men already resting. Well, except for the sickening smell. I found nine dead bodies laid in a row, as if ready for burial. Judging by the stench, this was not the first night they had lain there. A few steps further on there were three dead mules.

The dead men were probably Mac-Paps—so many of our comrades were reported as missing during that Aragon battle. The fighting was so savage that many were mutilated beyond recognition. We did not wear dog tags, so there was no way to know who they were.

We rested between the dead men and the dead mules until the scouts returned with reports of the enemy positions. When the order to move was finally whispered, we fled with lightning speed from that ravine of bloated dead.

Our squad was led to our next day's position, about two hundred yards from the outskirts of Azuara, and separate from the battalion, with orders to dig in. We needed the two hours to daybreak to get a trench dug down at least four feet so we would have some protection when enemy planes came over and their artillery opened up.

Here I would like to say a few words about the men in my unit. I could not have wished for a better outfit of comrades to have fighting at my side. In fact, throughout the war, I found myself with comrades I trusted and admired for their courage and discipline.

Being a light machine-gun unit, we were six in number: Corporal Amedee "Frenchy" Grenier, a French-Canadian, led the squad. He was noted for his quiet courage and able leadership and left Spain as a confirmed sergeant, with one of the finest records of any man.

The first gunner, "Blacky" Sanborn, an American, was to receive a present later that day from the enemy—a bullet passed through one his lungs and put him out of action for the rest of the war. He lived to get back to the United States where he had been a seaman before volunteering in Spain.

The second gunner, myself, needs no comment other than to say that I was an English-born Canadian, ashamed of the British government's betrayal of the democratic rights of the Spanish people. Their decision not to intervene disgusted me.

Brothers, Raymond and Stanley Henderson, were ammunition carriers, the latter with a quiet demeanour who obeyed orders without a murmur. In a few weeks, Stanley would be killed instantly with a bullet through the brain.

Stanley's brother, Ray, always seemed to be in the thick of it with me and won his right to be a sergeant on the battlefield. He was courageous and clear thinking and returned to Canada to carry on the fight for all that is decent in humanity.

The sixth of our unit, James Cameron, was cited for bravery in a later engagement, a very rare thing in the government forces. I knew no one else who received a medal for bravery. They were rarely given, even to officers. They received a card noting their leadership when they left Spain. Comrades who showed exceptional ability on the battlefield were sent to Officer Training School, providing the army with leaders who were trusted and respected by their comrades.

One Spanish lad was semi-officially attached to us as a runner. He spoke enough English to understand us and relayed information to and from battalion headquarters. It was a particularly demanding job and one of the most important. I do not remember seeing him after the next day, so can only assume he was killed. He was a good lad. We were all very fond of him and missed him greatly.

Our efforts rewarded us by daybreak. We had dug a trench four feet deep and as narrow as possible to give us some protection from strafing by planes, which owing to our lack of anti-aircraft guns, were able to come down to within two hundred feet and give us merry hell. Narrow trenches also gave far better protection against artillery fire, because if the shell fell just behind or in front, we had less chance of getting hit except by rock fragments.

We did not stay long in that trench. The order reached us to go on a scouting expedition to find out what activity was going on over the brow of a low hill. Our unit was chosen because we were ahead of the battalion, and a little to the left, giving us the best chance to reach the spot.

The squad was put under the command of Sergeant Owen D'Arcy, an American.[43] We went forward in open formation, with the sergeant in the lead. At ten yards apart, with only one man up at any one time, we would up and dash for a hollow in the ground or to a shallow spot in between so that on the next dash we could make it to better protection.

It took us about fifteen minutes to cover the first hundred yards. The terrain was of a gentle, rolling nature, and we were on a narrow flat going toward an upward slope. Only the odd shot greeted us from the left flank. As we reached the foot of the slope, twenty-five enemy planes flew overhead, forcing us to lay flat and keep our heads down while they bombed the already ruined village of Azuara behind us. Then they machine gunned the wooded areas nearby.

Finally, we reached the top of the slope but could not see any movement, so we took measures to fool the enemy into showing its hand. It was rather risky, but we had trained for this. First, the sergeant stood up on the skyline for a split second to attract the enemy's attention. This prepared them for further movements. In turn, we each showed ourselves for an instant.

The fire that greeted us gave us the information we needed for our report. Five or six machine guns, accompanied by intense rifle fire, had opened up on our left flank. Only a few scattered rifle shots greeted us from the front. This meant the fascists had started an encircling movement, leaving just enough soldiers in front to hold our battalion with aid from their artillery and planes.

We were able to reach our trench by noon without a single casualty, and were at once given orders to return to our position and place our machine gun out on the left flank. The situation was getting serious, because the fascists were on higher ground and had begun to shoot lengthwise into the main trench of the machine-gun company.

Sergeant D'Arcy led us back and around to the position. The rolling landscape gave ample protection until we got to the point where we would have to be exposed to a wall of bullets for about a hundred yards. We were about a third of a mile to the left of the battalion and feeling kind of lonely despite the fact that about ten men behind us were acting as a communication line to company headquarters.

Orders soon arrived. We were to get our machine gun into position at the earliest possible moment regardless of the cost, meaning regardless of the risk to our own lives. The enemy was preparing to attack from our flank, and drastic action was needed to save a lot of other lives.

By peeping over the top of our hollow, we could see a pile of rocks on the flat terrain a hundred yards ahead. That was our objective, but I wondered if it was humanly possible to get the gun out. The enemy was laying down a "beaten path of fire," concentrating on that open spot, knowing that we would have to pass through it to get to our position.

This meant that our movements had been observed, that our intentions had been rightly thought out, and that all means would be used to stop us. The enemy knew that one machine gun out there would have decent cover and could stop their advance.

Enemy artillery did not open up on us because we were so close to their own troops—they would have suffered more than ourselves from shell fragments—and they were forced to withdraw over the hill for shelter. As it was, the enemy was advancing with no opposition. Our own battalion was unable to give us cover fire, because they were behind a low hill which prevented them from seeing the enemy advance. It was left for the seven of us to get that gun out the best way we could.

The order for the gun to go forward was given by Sergeant D'Arcy. That meant the first and second gunners had to move together so that, if one went down, the other could carry on. For a few seconds before the order, I had been taking peeps at the terrain and getting a mental picture of any humps and hollows that might afford some protection while moving toward the best spot to place the gun.

With the order to go, the sergeant on one side and myself on the other, Blacky, the gunner, started to dash. I will try to recall the sensation that went through me the moment I took the first step forward. Or can I describe it? My first thought was to hope that I did not get one in the guts, for a belly wound is not nice. From there, I hoped I would get a clean shot through the head. A guy goes out quick that way, without any mess.

Then I realized that I did not want to die, and using my imagination, I made myself as small as possible. Finally, I thought, *What the hell, those bastards can't kill me. I'll show them. I'll get to that rock pile even if I break my neck getting there.*

On the third step forward, Blacky went down and fell on the gun. I shouted, "Get off that gun, boy! For Christ's sake, don't go to sleep." I had to roll him over to get it and learnt later that he got a bullet through a lung. Out of the corner of my eye, I saw Sergeant D'Arcy go down with a bullet in the thigh. I retrieved the gun and away I went, zigzagging without stopping.

My mind and eyes were focused on the objective, except when I stumbled twice. I cursed myself for being a damned clumsy fool. The machine gun, plus the ammo, was a heavy load to carry. With bullets coming from both sides and flying everywhere, a hundred yards over the rough terrain was no easy task. If I had been fully sane, I would have had a much tougher time and may have played out halfway. I often wonder how I made it without getting hit.

Captain Rafael Brage, a Spanish-American football player, the company commander at that time and later brigade intelligence head, was watching the activity through field glasses from an observation post in the tower of a ruined village church in the village which served as company headquarters. He told me later that, when I stumbled, he thought I had been hit. Maybe the fascists did, too. Maybe those stumbles saved my life.

Once I reached the rocks, I threw myself down behind them, giving myself a foot or so of cover. I shut my eyes for a few seconds to relax and take control. My nerves were under a terrific strain. I was sweating, my eyes were blurred, and I was shaking like a leaf. I have no excuse for my condition other than to say that I am human—not a block of wood—and anybody not having the same sensations must have something wrong with their brain. At least I did not lose control of my bowels.

The fire was intense, and when I looked back, I saw D'Arcy belly crawling to cover, but my comrades had not been able to drag Blacky back. It had been only a minute since we started our dash to get the gun out. My heart was thumping like a jackhammer, but it was time to see what was in front of me. Raising myself a fraction, I saw something that drove all other thoughts from my mind.

Having received no return fire, the fascists had become bold—and very foolish. Five had come over the brow of the hill and were standing no more than two hundred yards from me, blazing away in our general direction. They must have received word from their observers that we were a small unit and had seen three of us go down. They did not know I had reached my goal. It is the only way to explain their nerve.

Along the skyline, at regular intervals, the enemy was giving us the same test we had given them that morning. They looked like a bunch of Jack-in-the-boxes. Some even gained enough confidence to stand out in the open or to kneel and fire.

My eyes were mainly attracted to the bold and foolish five, and it was on these that I settled. Everything was forgotten as I concentrated on what a surprise they were going to receive from a "dead or badly-wounded man."

I remember how I wiped the sweat from my eyes, how I drew the gun down to see that the barrel was not plugged, how I snapped the lever back and pulled the belt through—ejecting a shell to be sure the gun was properly loaded—how I adjusted the sights for the short range, and how I ensured the bipods were free.

I remember these actions as though I had done them yesterday.

Bullets were chipping splinters from the rocks as, keeping my head down, I edged the gun over the rock pile. Picking a moment when there was a lull in their fire, I raised my head and sighted on the group of five who had drawn together.

To save the ammunition, having only a hundred-round belt on the drum and not knowing if any of my comrades would be able to get out with more, I let go a burst of only five, then quickly ducked and peeped.

Two were down and three were running back. I took a snap at the runners with another short burst. I was rewarded with one more biting the dust. The others were over the hill before I could get another bead on them. I should mention that a man two hundred yards from a machine gun seems to be stuck on the barrel after one has been practising at half-mile ranges. They are easy marks.

I turned my attention to the skyline and let off about fifty rounds to quiet the others. The words, "You got three of 'em!" brought me back to earth. Ray Henderson and Frenchy Grenier had belly slid out under that murderous fire with more ammunition and a first-aid kit in case I was wounded.

Blacky and D'Arcy had made it back out of sight, and Stanley Henderson was lying about halfway, acting as a contact. We shouted back to let him know that everything was under control and not to come out because there was not enough cover for four.

Ray and Frenchy got busy sniping with their rifles, and soon only the odd shot came our way. After that, there was very little shooting because the enemy would have had to show themselves against the skyline. With my gun ready to blast at such reckless exposure, the enemy kept their nuts down.[44] [45]

To make things even better, one of our own machine guns opened up in the woods on our left, which let us know that guns on our side were moving into position on our flanks. We also received heartening news from company headquarters that the battalion was holding the line.

A smoke was the order of the day. Leaving the watch with Ray and Frenchy, I lay on my back and relaxed.

Chapter 8
SURROUNDED BY FASCISTS[46]

THE REST OF THAT day, there was a terrific bombardment by planes and artillery on the Mac-Paps in the main trench. Clouds of dust and smoke completely hid the area. We had good reason to be thankful we were safe in "no-man's land" and wondered how many of our comrades would live through it. At dusk, one of our own artillery fired two shots—the only shots fired by the heavy stuff on our side all day.

At dark, we ceased fire and sent our patrols to guard against surprise attacks. The enemy came over the hill and started digging in, and we sent back for a pick and shovel to do the same. We took turns with digging and guarding until midnight, at which time we were ordered to withdraw.

We received some bread and stew—we needed it—and joined the rest of the machine-gun company, or what was left of it. We found one or two of our friends and heard how so-and-so got his and who had been wounded. In all, there were sixty-three left of the hundred and thirty that went into action that morning.

By now, it was the battalion's third night with no sleep and no orders. Finally, at midnight, the battalion received the order to retire, from what had turned out to be the seventh runner to be sent. The others I never saw again. They were either killed, wounded or captured.

Carrying our arms, we moved to the heights behind the village of Azuara, a journey that took two hours over difficult terrain. During this retreat, we passed through the village, a place where people had once lived, where the women washed and gossiped the year 'round—a sight that now would have turned the most forgiving and tender heart to hate against those whose god was destruction.

After climbing over the hump nearest the village, thence down and over a couple of other hills, we received the order to rest and picked the softest rocks for a bed. Within an hour, we started to move again. Slipping and sliding up and down hills, we made our torturous way in the dark, not knowing where we were going, but hoping our guides at least knew the general direction. It was just a matter of following the comrade in front and finding the best footholds on the trail.

It was breaking day when at last we halted in what we thought was our retreat position. An enemy battalion had been spotted, and we waited until their position had been determined. Rifle fire and the odd machine-gun blast gave us the clue. We were walking right into them! Their advance the day before had been so great around our flanks that we found ourselves encircled. The only way open was to make for the village of Lecera. We needed to move quickly before the enemy cut us off completely. We moved in small units, and any who could not keep up were to join the unit behind.

The rest of the battalion had retired, and a dozen or so of us were left behind to try to hold the enemy if they used the road to advance further in that direction. By some chance of fate, I did not have anybody assigned to me, as did the other two machine gunners. I was alone with my gun and had fallen behind. Hoping to catch up, I took an overland shortcut to avoid a curve in the road and missed a truck that had been ordered to dump its supplies and pick up any machine gunners. Eventually, they saw me struggling to reach the road and picked me up as well.

After a mile or so, we were let off the truck, told the direction to go, and were on our own to find our way to the rear. The day was scorching hot, and we had about ten or twelve miles to go over rough terrain. I was thirsty, the gun seemed to weigh a ton, and it was impossible for me to keep up.

Eventually, I came to a muddy pool where six comrades were soaking their feet and taking mouthfuls of the putrid water. One was straining the stuff through a shirt and taking sips, though he would have been warned of the danger of drinking it. I took mouthfuls and gargled, keeping the water in my mouth for a few seconds to refresh myself before spitting it out.

After soaking my swollen feet and sloshing water over my head, I laid down in cover of the brush with my feet elevated to get the blood back to the top part of my body. I was told by one of the comrades that the five other men were from another brigade—maybe Germans or Italians fighting for the Republic— and they, like us, had lost track of their outfit during the withdrawal. Staying only long enough to cool off, I resumed my trek to find my own outfit, staying in the cover, and keeping the sun over my left shoulder so I would know I was going in the right direction.

I came to a spot where I would be exposed for about half a mile and searched for movement while I rested in the shade. Seeing nothing, I started across the open space carrying the gun with the ammo belt tied around my middle, ready for action.

I had just reached the cover of a wooded area when I noticed someone I could not see properly coming toward me on a horse. I aimed my gun just as I heard my name and recognized the voice. It was José Medina, captain of the Mac-Pap machine-gun company.

"Relax, Jim, and take your finger off that trigger!" I was aiming the gun right at him, and he was more than a little disturbed. He had me mount the horse with the gun and took the reins.

He told some of us later that the encounter was the closest he ever came to being killed by one of his own men, let alone a good friend. He was sure that, if I had not known the sound of his voice, I would have let go and asked questions afterwards.

I have often thought of that moment and have concluded that, in that instant, my brain was sending out signals without me realizing it. My manual responses had been keyed up to action—indeed a very fast reaction—but I had not pressed the trigger. But then, how can anyone explain what happens in a split second.

Captain Medina was the sort of officer soldiers dream about commanding them but seldom do. I had been in some tough situations with him, and we saved one another's lives more than once. I was shifted around so much that most of the time I did not know where I was or who the comrades were who were fighting with me. He was a constant presence, and I will always consider him the best officer I had alongside me in battle.

When I first arrived in Spain, some of the officers were political selections who I would not trust in battle. In two cases, I had firsthand knowledge that they deserted the comrades who were depending on them for leadership. Anyway, Medina was one who could be trusted and any in his command would follow him to the "gates of hell."

On the trip back to the nut grove, Captain Medina filled me in. A reserve republican brigade had engaged the enemy on the left flank, relieving our troops so that they could retire to the rear. He had been ordered to find anyone who had been encircled and came across a unit that had been attacked by planes. Only one of the six men was alive. Medina had sent him to the rear along with the comrade who was helping him with the search. That was when he found me.

When I rejoined my comrades, I was given bread, a tin of bully beef, and muddy coffee laced with cognac. As soon as I finished cleaning my gun, the order came to move into a village a short distance off, where a first-aid post had been set up in a church. The fascists may have been bombing the churches, but stone walls were strong so they were good for this purpose. Any seriously wounded were taken by truck to hospitals in cities on the coast.

A keg of wine was found and Captain Medina gave me the task of guarding it. We usually drank wine because most water was contaminated. Hardly able to keep my eyes open, I was to make sure none received too much. In their weakened condition, too much would not have been helpful. We could not afford to lose any of the eighty or so men that remained. I knew only two, and they helped me when some complained at my refusal to give them what I felt was too much. One comrade made more of a fuss, but the others dealt with him by reminding him why he had come to Spain.

Only half of us had weapons. The rest had abandoned them in the chaos of the Retreats. I am not blaming them. In the condition some of these men were in, even a rifle was a burden.

This time, though, I was in possession of the only machine gun and some wondered how I had managed to hold onto it. I did leave my packsack with an officer to be sent on to brigade headquarters. I felt the gun was all I could manage.[47]

The pack contained the personal effects I always carried, along with a loaf of dried-out bread. There was some material I had to keep, because it was secret, but I knew what to do if there was any chance of being captured. By letting the pack go, I relieved myself of about three pounds. I was never to see that pack again.

A message arrived ordering me to get on a truck for another mission, but first, I was to see that any leftover wine was dumped after canteens and skins were filled for those who could use it wisely. I filled my own canteen and was thankful I had done so before another night set in. The truck had food, ammo, and side arms, and on the way, besides a few others, the driver picked up Ray, Frenchy, and Cameron, along with two young Spanish lads we knew. We sure were glad to be together again.

As we left the village, planes were thick in the sky and shells began to land around us as we took up a position on the outskirts. Trenches had already been dug and a couple of machine-gun posts had been prepared—a good thing, because I was bone tired after several days of unrelenting battle. Tired, tired, tired.

It was getting dusk, and tanks could be seen advancing on the village. We set up the two machine guns, waited for the tanks to get closer, and opened fire. Then we heard rifle fire we did not know was with us, and later learnt that three Spanish companies were nearby. They were the ones who had prepared the position.

During the night, we set up my gun in three different positions and kept our fire on the tanks that could be seen faintly in the dark. Although it was too dark to be accurate with our fire, we managed to stop their advances.

A couple of times during the night, we were ordered to stop firing while our Spanish comrades belly wormed out to three tanks that had not moved since our first shots. We saw the explosions as they tossed anti-tank bombs into the treads of each tank. They were no good after that.

Before dawn, we were ordered to retire. Stumbling around, with patrols ahead and on our flanks, we passed through the deserted village, and by daybreak, the twelve of us with our rifles and two machine guns, were camped alone in a ravine. The Spanish companies had been led somewhere else.

We received rations of bread, canned meat, and jam (a rare commodity). I do not know where they got that jam; maybe from the enemy. I filled my canteen with wine, since I had shared mine with my unit during the night. There must have been some good organizing to have food ready for us.

We cleaned our guns and checked our ammo. An hour or so later, Captain Medina arrived with a Spanish officer. We learnt that the Spanish battalion's machine-gun squads had not arrived to back up their rifle companies as expected, and Medina had received the call for help from a Spanish captain. Though he knew we were dead on our feet, he had sent us in to fill the gap. A few in the Spanish unit had been wounded by shrapnel but none killed. After thanking us, the Spanish officer left.

About nine that morning, we started to move in open formation in cover of the wood along the road. We were ten yards apart, except for those of us with machine guns who had our ammo carriers close by. We passed around a village where a line of defence was to be dug to hold the enemy until a stronger fortification could be prepared in the rear.

We could hear planes bombing our side's trenches that morning, along with enemy artillery pounding away. Medina told me later that the Spanish comrades had put clothes on sticks so the trenches would appear occupied to spotter planes. They sure used up tons of explosives without a single kill.

We halted a mile outside the village for a short rest. The location was ideal, with good cover and a small stream. Spreading out, no less than ten yards apart, we stripped off our clothes and started killing lice eggs—nit picking—in the seams of our pants and other parts of our so-called uniforms, mostly khaki outerwear that more or less fitted.

Someone had a large bar of laundry soap, about ten inches long, which he cut into six pieces for sharing. Laundry soap was worth its weight in gold. Each battalion dished this out once a month, but owing to the fact that most of our group had not been at rest with our battalions at the rear for some time, we had not received any soap, or pay for that matter (although there was nothing to spend it on).

We bathed and gave our pants a good washing. Refreshed, we put on our wet clothes and continued on. It was a hot day, and they dried in a couple of hours.

Ray Henderson was my second gunner, and we took turns carrying the gun and ammo. The captain knew we would not be able to keep up, so we were told to stay under cover and follow a trail beside the road that was taking us in the right direction. The machine gun we were lugging was a heavy maxim, a water-cooled model, and though without wheels or armour shield, it was still quite a weight to carry for any length of time, around sixty pounds.

We heard a jeep coming but took no chances. While Ray covered me with the gun, I stepped out from the trail and showed myself, pistol at the ready. The jeep stopped, and the driver blurted that José Medina had sent him back to give us a lift. I called to Ray that it was okay.

The driver, Jack Matthews, was attached to brigade headquarters.[48] He told us the rest of our outfit had met up with a larger group on the same mission and had told the commander about our plight with the heavy gun.

On the way back, Jack told us he had been warned that we would be very cautious, but even so, we had scared the hell out of him.

Chapter 9
THE CROSSROAD

DURING THIS NEXT ACTION, I was listed as missing in the Retreats. Three days later, I was found and taken to 15th Brigade Headquarters where I was put in a jeep to an unknown destination. Here is the story.[49]

I had been transferred from the Mac-Pap machine-gun company to the 15th Brigade's machine-gun unit.[50] This unit gave the brigade the flexibility to send machine-gun squads wherever they were needed by any of its battalions. In this case, the brigade had received information from our planes that the enemy was moving up heavy war materials, and I was ordered to cover a crossroad.[51] Their object was to encircle the Mac-Pap battalion, which was digging in about three hundred yards to the rear of the position we were to take up.

I picked twenty-four comrades, the best men, who knew me well. These were men I could depend on. Such was our discipline and comradeship that if any one of us needed help, the others would be there to aid him. Three were Spaniards who could make themselves understood in English—especially the curse words—but the outfit consisted mostly of English-speaking men from all countries. Few would come out of this action alive.

We did not use dog tags, and the only identifying insignia we wore were small patches on our berets that could be disposed of if there was any chance of capture. There was a good reason for this method of identification: A badge or stripes on the coat would leave a light area on the cloth if anything was ripped off before capture.

I sent and received messages from brigade headquarters by going through the Mac-Paps as an intermediary. The field telephones were unreliable, so "runners" on motorcycles received and passed on information from battalion headquarters to the brigade staff, who would in turn relay orders back to our unit, that is, if the runners could reach us.

On this mission, our unit had three guns, one of them heavy, without its shield or wheels. It was water cooled and stood on a tripod. The other two were light with round drums of ammunition. Each contained up to a hundred rounds.

I had a crude hand-drawn map identifying where we were to position ourselves on a cliff overlooking the crossroad. It showed the area to be covered about two hundred yards south of our position. The map indicated steep sixty-degree inclines on the south, east, and west sides. The north had a twenty-degree easy slope back through shrubs and trees where the battalion was digging in, and also fortifying both sides of the road that led north from the crossroad.

Arriving at the top, we found very little cover. It was four hundred feet up and mainly solid rock. It was apparent that we would not be able to see the crossroad unless we came up to the brink. We gathered together in the cover of trees to discuss the situation and decided that four of us would belly crawl, twelve yards apart, to the ridge. Canadian Ray Henderson and I took the centre and the other two took the flanks.

Before we left our cover, Ray signalled me by pointing up. We called to our comrades on the flanks to stop and lay still. Ray and I used our field glasses to check a single-engine plane headed toward us. I was not concerned about the rest of the group, because I had left Stanley, Ray's brother, in charge and knew they were spread out in the cover.

It was an observation plane, and we knew the pilot had small contact bombs he could throw over the side if he saw any movement on the ground. He would also have a radio to relay our position to their gunners. Luckily, our group had not been noticed as the pilot looked over the side only a few feet above the hill. After the plane flew over, we crawled to the ridge and saw the target. Shortly after, we heard explosions and rifle shots where I figured the battalion was to our rear.

We decided to try to shoot the plane down on its return, and Ray went back to get a machine gun. When the plane came back, we could see that it had been hit by rifle fire. Ray stood up and held the legs of the gun on his shoulders, while I knelt down and aimed up at the plane. I hit it with three short bursts, and it nose-dived in flames at the bottom of the cliff. The ejected shell casings slipped down Ray's neck and burnt him, so I sent him back to our first-aid man, and as it was getting dusk, I told him to send the rest of the unit up.

Not wanting to attract attention to our position, we did not fire on the enemy soldiers who went out to the burning plane. Instead, we kept ourselves busy tying down the three guns and aiming them at the crossroad, only a hundred yards down from us as the crow flies. We placed the guns thirty yards apart and checked and double-checked the sightings. The legs were firmly entrenched between rocks; the only possible movement was a fraction of an inch up or down.

Three of the comrades volunteered to go back to the battalion to get us some grub before it got dark. They brought back a pot of stew, bread, and what was called coffee. Some of the food was taken to the three who were watching the guns and checking on enemy movements.

We ate, had the first smoke in three hours, and spread out under cover to rest until the guards sent back information that activity had started on the target. We did not need the runner to tell us that. We heard trucks and armour coming, moving very slowly without lights, but they had not yet reached the crossroad.

The rumblings went on for about ten minutes. They were close, but we could not see anything except what was lit up by the burning plane. Suddenly, Ray gripped my arm and pointed. A hooded flashlight was moving back and forth at the crossroad. Waiting a minute, until I was sure they were going north, I told Ray to fire a short burst while I looked through the glasses.

I saw the flashlight arc and seemingly fall to the ground. "The gun is dead on! You must have hit the guide!" Moving to the gun on my left, I told the gunner to let off a short burst. I watched and thought the gun should be elevated. Ray, who was watching through his glasses, agreed and the muzzle was elevated a fraction before the gunner shot off another short burst. While we watched, we heard the bullets hitting on steel, probably a tank.

Though it was dark, light from the stars and burning plane showed that the column had stopped, and as our fire had been so short, they had not pinpointed our position. Ray and I went to the gun on the right and had them centre it in the same way.

Suddenly, an enemy flare lit up the area. Peering over the ridge, we saw them. In the lead was a tank followed by six trucks, then another tank with more trucks behind it. The soldiers had left the trucks, and we could see movement behind them. Two more flares went up. Suddenly, their artillery sent a barrage over our heads aimed to our left, and we realized their flares had given them the location of our three pieces of heavy artillery. First World War stuff most likely. That's when our own artillery started firing over us toward the crossroad. Their sixth shell hit smack on target, setting two enemy trucks on fire.

The other tanks and trucks were contoured by the light of the burning trucks, but we only fired one gun at a time to keep from being spotted. Then we saw that the enemy were moving left at the crossroad. I took over Ray's gun while he sent a runner to tell the battalion that the enemy had changed direction.

Suddenly, a shell from one of our own heavy guns fell short and exploded on the gun to my right, killing five members of my outfit. I sent word back to battalion headquarters, reporting what had happened and giving the names of the dead.

We kept up our fire, trying to conserve the ammo we had. Two runners who were sent back for instructions did not return. Later, a squad arrived to bury the five that were killed. At dawn, we had only two drums of ammo left for the one light gun, and we decided to quit shooting until we received orders from battalion headquarters. We waited all morning under the trees and could hear firing behind us, but no word came.

Four other comrades who had been wounded by shrapnel from the stray shell were taken to the rear. Counting the two runners who had not returned, we were down to six men. I sent another comrade back to learn what our orders were.

I discussed the situation with the five who were left, and we decided to withdraw as there was already lots of shooting between us and the battalion. Three picked up the light gun and moved back. Ray and I carried the heavy water-cooled gun and the canister of ammo, keeping the weapon loaded.

We had gone about fifty yards when we heard a burst of rifle fire along with a few rounds from our own light gun, then only rifle shots. Ray took my pistol and binoculars and belly crawled around the bend in the path to see what had happened.

Within a minute, I saw him coming back. "Our men are all dead, and they are using their bodies for target practice," he said angrily. "We are going to be dead ourselves if we try to get out that way!"

It had started to rain and was growing dark. We knew we had to escape. We picked up the hand grenades, and pulling the pins, threw them down the side of the cliff where we could hear the enemy shooting. Then we slid and crawled down the other side, hauling our gun and ammo with us.

The rain increased, and it was dark when we finally reached the bottom. I knew from the hand-drawn map that the ravine was a route to the rear toward friendly forces, so we followed it, plodding along with short rests every hour or so. We had no idea how far we went that night, but by keeping to where the growth was thickest, we sensed we were going in the right direction.

By now, we had not slept for three days. At daybreak, as wet as we were, we fell into an exhausted sleep. Early in the afternoon, I woke Ray and we went looking for food. Everything was silent nearby, but we heard guns booming off to our right. A short distance away, we saw a peasant's hut and three goats. We watched the area for half an hour through our field glasses, and except for a man and woman, there was no activity.

We wormed our way as close as we could without exposing ourselves. I was ready to go to the hut to see if I could buy some food when Ray said, "Look Jim, I can make myself understood in Spanish much better than you. I'll go while you cover me." I had to agree, so giving him my side arm, I covered him while he went to the hut.

Ray walked the twenty yards, and the man came out and invited him inside. Within ten minutes, Ray came back to where I was sitting out of sight. He had been lucky and had cheese, a loaf of bread, two oranges, and a goatskin full of wine. We went a mile or so before we stopped to eat most of the bread and cheese, washing it down with wine.

Ray told me the people had not asked questions and refused payment for the food, but he insisted on giving them a hundred pesetas. They thought he was alone and told him there were no troops in the area.

It was still raining, so after a rest, we decided to keep moving. We had not gone far, maybe a couple of miles, when we heard a group of men talking English. We walked up and asked the one who seemed to be in charge to take us to the officer in command. Ray unloaded the gun, and I was amazed when I saw the canister was empty. We only had six rounds left.

Ray admitted that he had known this the whole time but did not think it wise to let me know as he felt I had enough to think about in getting us to safety. I told the comrade that my name was Jim and that my partner was Ray, not giving any last names. He understood and introduced us to the other three in the same manner. I took my beret out of my pocket and motioned to Ray to do the same.

The captain in command knew me but had not been informed of my special assignment. After a short chat, he picked up the field telephone and asked to be connected with brigade headquarters. It took about ten minutes before he got through. After talking briefly, he handed me the phone. The person on the other end told me that the captain had been ordered to send us to the rear on the first transport available. That's how we came to be taken to brigade headquarters in an ambulance.

There, we were transferred to a jeep, with all on board armed with side arms and rifles. It took about three hours to reach our final destination, and it was dusk when we finally went through a village and stopped at a large stone farmhouse a mile outside. There were many guards around—I spotted a few after we had left the village—and all were partially hidden. We were greeted by a guard, and the driver turned over the order papers and left.

We were escorted into a large room that served as a kitchen and fed a stew containing cabbage, garbanzos, and goat meat, along with some bread. This was the first real meal we had eaten for some time.

We finished and waited until we were sent into another room, where officers and their aides were giving and receiving orders over half a dozen phones. I recognized two officers who had taken part in the special instruction school and realized we were in the headquarters of the 5th Army Corps.[52] They glanced at me and lifted their hands in acknowledgement.

One of them rose and motioned us to take a seat. He said that he had been ordered to find out why we had not received the retirement order sent to us by brigade headquarters via the Mac-Paps. He let us know that, after receiving my reports of the enemy's change of direction, and of one of our shells killing five and wounding four, the battalion had sent us an order to retire.

We told him the order never reached us, and that we sent three runners back but nobody returned. We also told him what happened to the three comrades who went back just ahead of us and that we were the only two left when we decided to retire.

Finally, he told us that we were going to the coast for a few days to relax, and we would receive orders when the leave finished. Each afternoon, we were to report to a post in the city. Stanley Henderson and another comrade, Nick Myers, had somehow got back to the battalion, and were reporting at the same time.

Chapter 10
CAPTURE AND ESCAPE

"ONLY HEAVEN" KNEW WHERE I was. It seemed I was the only living person in that mountainous area. We were still in the March 1938 Retreats, and I had lost track of my comrades. I had no food or drink and existed on grass and fallen olives. They were dried up but at least they were something to chew and swallow.[53] [54]

On the third day, I dismantled my light machine gun and threw away parts as I moved, to prevent the enemy finding it in one piece. I could carry it no more. At some point, I got rid of my pistol. By now, the fourth or fifth day, I was exhausted and out of touch with reality. I had fallen down and figured this was the end. Somebody would find me dead.

I am recalling this forty years after it happened. It has been lost to me all this time, but now I am remembering it as though it happened yesterday. It is all so clear. Why? And I am now remembering that, more than once in Spain, I had been in the same condition.

The only weapons I had left at the time of my collapse were two hand grenades. I hid them and lay down. Hiding the grenades was a wise thing to do, because if the enemy found you with weapons, you were shot on the spot. I have no idea how long I was in that sprawling position before I heard voices and got a kick in the ribs. The first word that escaped my lips was, "*Agua.*" Water. I soon realized I was in enemy hands, a captive.

After being slapped about the face, I opened my eyes and saw two soldiers standing over me. I knew they were enemy soldiers, because they were smartly dressed. The Republican Army did not have smart uniforms, except for the generals. I was given wine from a canteen, pulled to my feet, dragged to a truck, and thrown in the back.

I lost consciousness again and came to in an olive grove. It was raining like hell and four other prisoners shared their stew with me.[55] I noticed a sound that gave me hope: rushing water. This meant we were camped beside a river. I was fed again, came back to the land of the living, and began to take stock.

There were seven enemy soldiers, including an officer, guarding five of us prisoners. Two of our captors were on guard, and the rest were billeted in a peasant's hut. One of the prisoners was Bob Dyer, a Canadian from Winnipeg.[56] The other three were from Spanish brigades. Bob told me he had been captured the day before, and that our guards were awaiting orders to transfer us to a larger unit where we would have no chance of escape. The guards were about ten yards away, on the landward side, which meant we were closer to the river.

Shivering with cold and wet, we laid our plans. Bob had seen the river, about thirty feet away. It was the Ebro, in flood after three days of steady rain. We knew that, if we could get to the other side, we would be safe in Republican territory. Considering the weather conditions, and the chance of being shot in the back, we decided that the best time to go would be just after the change of guards at midnight.

We could tell the guards were mainly interested in keeping themselves comfortable under a waterproof garment. We also knew that, rather than go to the trouble of taking us back to their command, they would just as soon shoot us for trying to escape.

Right after the guard change, we took off our footwear and jackets, hung them around our necks, and slowly belly crawled to the river. We could hardly see our hands before our eyes. Bob told me he was not much of a swimmer, and I (in my weakened state) was not much better. I advised him not to use up his energy trying to swim across but to relax and let the river float us downstream.

We slid into the water and took a few strokes to get into the current, which quickly floated us down the river. I have no idea how long we continued this way before Bob, who was holding onto me, developed a cramp and started to clutch desperately. I found myself in trouble but managed to break his hold and grabbed him from the rear.

In England, I had received intensive training in lifesaving, right to the point where a fellow swimming-club member would simulate a drowning person. Every morning at five o'clock, for a month, I was taught how to break holds. It was not a game; whoever dragged me under was instructed how to vigorously fight any hold.

For the first few days of this training, I would have drowned along with the person I was supposed to save. More than once we were pulled exhausted from the pool and received lifesaving attention for real while we gasped and spluttered. It was tough, but that training saved me to write this.

Of course, the conditions Bob and I found ourselves in were very different from that indoor swimming pool. While I was in the river, I was weak and numb with cold, but at least we were in a current that was sweeping us toward the shore we wanted to reach. As we got close, the water became less than five feet deep, but it was impossible to keep our feet on the bottom because of the strong current. I had all but given up when suddenly we were carried into a back eddy at a bend in the river.

I found strength from somewhere to drag Bob to shore. Spewing as much water out of myself as I could, I turned my attention to Bob and pumped him out until he started gasping for air. The last thing I remember, before becoming unconscious, was Bob holding my hand and murmuring, "Thanks."

When I came to, I was being given brandy and somebody was slapping my face. A voice called, "He's come out of it!" I rolled my head to one side and saw that I was in a stone farm building with a blazing fire in a big fireplace. I had been stripped of my lice-ridden rags and was wrapped in three blankets. I felt warm and comfortable. At that point, I did not remember the escape and had no idea where I was. Somebody started feeding me soup, and talking to keep me awake.

Somebody else bent over me and told me to relax and try to think of the last thing I remembered. He told me where I was, that I had been there for two days, and that while I was unconscious, I had been talking. He also said that I had a name tattooed on my left arm. Then I was left alone.

After collecting my thoughts, I told them of the escape and asked after Bob. I was told I had been found alone but evidence showed that I must have had somebody with me, as they found footwear and a jacket about twenty feet away. A thorough search had been made, but no other trace of Bob could be found.

The unit that found me was one of the small search-and-rescue outfits that were set up during the Retreats. I was sent to the rear and hospitalized for a couple of days before being reunited with what was left of the brigade's special machine-gun outfit.[57] In the next few weeks, with every unit I was in touch with, I asked the same question, "Have you any knowledge of Bob Dyer?" I always came up with a negative answer.

Chapter 11
DEATH OF A COMRADE[58]

THE MAC-PAPS HAD BEEN at rest after the fierce fighting of March but were not up to full strength as the losses had been heavy. On the afternoon of March 31, we received orders to move back to the front; the enemy had broken through our lines with a flanking movement.

As the first to move, machine-gun squads from all companies were ordered to leave their units and commandeer any empty trucks to take them as close as possible to the front. Around five o'clock, with the help of a Spanish lieutenant, our squad—myself, Ray Henderson, Stanley Henderson, Claude Nash, Tommy Roberts, Tommy Blackburn, and Frenchy Grenier—was able to get a lift on an old truck.

It was getting dusk by the time we reached a crossroad that had to be held at least a day to give fleeing civilians time to move to the rear, and at the same time giving government forces time to move in much needed supplies. Our squad's operation was to help keep this route open.

Our truck turned at the crossroad, and we made our way toward the front. The road was full of bomb holes, and though it was now dark, we were driving without lights as a precaution against enemy reconnaissance planes.

Suddenly, the truck lurched onto its side; we had come to grief in a bomb crater in the centre of the road. I was on the low side of the truck, and one of the comrades had thrown his arms out to grab at anything that would save him being thrown out. It happened to be my throat, and I had to suffer his panicked clutch while the boys on top untangled themselves.

Just when I figured I had seen all the stars and flashes one sees before the lights goes out for good, the pressure lifted, and I fell out of the truck. I must have been out cold for a minute or so, because when I looked around, the rest of the comrades had already picked up their equipment and were ready to move. I was helped to my feet, my gun handed to me, and we started forward on foot.

Along the road to the front, we met hundreds of women, children, and old people trekking to the rear. Their homes had been razed to the ground by fascist bombs. It is hard to tell of my feelings as they passed us, moaning and crying. Hate was uppermost in my mind—hate for those responsible for the murder of non-combatants.

The burnt bodies of wounded being taken to the rear were still in trucks that had been bombed and strafed during the afternoon. They had been struck by incendiary bombs and roasted alive. Later, I stopped to take a bloody mess from the arms of an injured woman sitting on the side of the road. It was a baby, or what had been a baby. The vacant stare she gave me will stay with me the rest of my life.[59]

At some point, we were told to occupy a line of trenches that had already been dug, and we spread out in search of them. This was no easy matter in the dark. Finally, word reached us that the fascists had already occupied them.

It was now our business to make new positions and trust that, when daylight came, we would find ourselves with good cover and within firing range. When day broke, it turned out my gun was facing an olive grove, and I had to move it to higher ground. We were able to dig down behind a rock by the time activities opened.

The sun rose slowly, sending a glow over enemy-occupied territory as fascist observation planes came over in search of our defences. We laid flat and ceased all movement, as their reports could give enemy gunners their range. With no fortifications and no heavy field guns of our own in the rear to return the fire, it was far wiser to let their land forces do the spotting.

The first shot that morning blasted off just behind me. For a brief moment, I thought the enemy had managed to get behind us during the night. Actually, it was a boy from Winnipeg. His rifle had been caught in the brush and he had given it an extra yank as he pulled it out by the barrel. The trigger snapped back. Boom! Away went half his hand.

A well-trained soldier would not have done that, but by now there was often no time for proper training before someone was sent into battle. It was just a matter of shoving him up to the front line and telling him to keep his head down.

Shortly after, the enemy opened up a barrage of heavy artillery on our open positions. They were about fifteen hundred yards ahead, and I could see the flashes of their light field guns blasting away at us. I reported back on their position, in the meantime sending streams of lead in their direction.

The light Maxim I was firing got too hot and a shell casing broke off in the breech. Without a tool to take the casing out, I was forced to take the gun down—disassemble it—and put in a new barrel. We were lucky, because Ray had managed to snag an extra barrel the day before.

With shells bursting all around, I dismantled the gun but was in too much of a hurry and burnt my hand, though it was more my vanity that was wounded. Fancy a guy being so damned foolish as to grab a red-hot barrel, especially after having taken the gun down hundreds of times without touching a cold barrel, even while blindfolded. Everyone had a good laugh about it afterwards.

Soon we discovered we had no protection on our flanks. The enemy had got well behind us and were firing on us from both sides. We were pretty well surrounded, and they were closing in. This was a hell of a spot to be in. We received the order to retire and moved back slowly, making stands in small groups wherever cover could be found.

Stanley Henderson was the second gunner, and he stayed with me with the extra ammo. The machine gun was light, weighing only about forty pounds. It was the type that usually stays with the infantry and is used to cover the retirement of the main body of the company. When the company gets back to some kind of cover, the company riflemen start firing to cover the machine gun's retirement. In this way, we gradually made our way back. Tommy Blackburn lost our group at this point, and we learnt later that he had been captured.

We took a second stand in a small olive grove on a hillside and kept the fascists off until they blasted hell out of our position with trench mortars and artillery. The riflemen were ordered back again because only thirteen remained of Company 3, the Mac-Pap Machine-Gun Company. Ray, Stan, and I, along with a few others, were covering them when the enemy found our range with their trench mortars. At the first barrage, six of our boys were killed and most of the others wounded.

When the rest had retired, Ray followed in their direction while Stan and I picked up the gun with the ammo still lodged in it and started to move. At that moment, Stan was shot through the head and fell on the ammo. I went down with him, the bullet grazing my nose before passing through his left temple, a little above the ear, and exiting out the right temple.

I shouted to Ray to come back, and he helped me roll his brother off the ammunition box. Making sure Stanley was dead, we made tracks to get out, somehow dodging bullets and shrapnel. I felt a few burns but soon forgot them.[60]

The company's last move, though short as the crow flies, had been over a mile owing to the terrain and the need to zigzag for cover. Having travelled half the distance, we came upon what was meant to be our breakfast: coffee and oranges.

This was luck indeed, and we stopped long enough to fill our shirts with oranges but changed our minds about drinking the coffee due to a certain lack of understanding between us and the fascists; just as Ray tipped the coffee barrel over, a burst of machine-gun fire filled it full of holes. How Ray was missed cannot be explained.

A little further along, we met up with Tommy Roberts, and as we approached what had been brigade headquarters, we came upon Claude Nash, Frenchy Grenier, and our commander, Captain Brage. He was damned glad to see us, thinking we had been captured or killed. He told us we were completely cut off from the rest of our forces and went to the top of the hill with glasses to see if there was any opening we might be able to sneak through.

In the meantime, we set up the gun, and gave all enemy mass movements as much trouble as possible. Captain Brage returned and instructed us to follow him, keeping as far apart as possible. For six hundred yards or so, everything was okay. We kept to the north side of the hill where the growth was thickest but then had to run a gauntlet of crossfire where the enemy were closing the gap of the encirclement.

We got through and after an hour of twisting and turning, always keeping in the valley and in the trees, we finally made contact with the rest of the battalion, or what was left of it; about eighty men who were trying to dig a defence line between shots. Among those that were missing were three of my comrades from Saskatoon: George Thomas, Shorty Edward Gilroy (Irving), and Pat Pritchard. As for my company, other than Ray Henderson and Tommy Roberts, I could find only two left.

Our small group of Canadians held the enemy at bay till dusk. While we were holding the position, we repulsed a tank attack. The tanks got to within a hundred yards of us before our fire stopped them. The bullets must have given them quite a concussion. Imagine yourself in a drum with somebody banging on it.

When the seventh tank stopped, the inmates got out and took cover behind it. I was shooting our gun while Ray held the legs on his shoulders. Otherwise, it would have been too low. I had just finished a belt and was looking around for Tommy Roberts, who was loading the other belt, when I chanced to see Tom Ewen, a youngster from Vancouver, trying to light a tank bomb with the idea of throwing it at the tanks. The distance was too far, but I don't suppose he knew that. The bomb was in the shape of a cylinder with a fuse that must be split a little at the top before being lit. He did not know this, either.

Suddenly, he jumped up and, waving the bomb above his head, shouted, "Who the bloody hell knows how to light this thing!" Bullets and shrapnel were flying pretty thick, but Tom Ewen was too vexed to notice. I am writing this with a smile, but at the time it was not so damned amusing. By dusk, we had run out of ammunition and what was left of the battalion retreated. We had not eaten since dinner the day before but a body forgets about food at such times.

The next day, April second, we held up the enemy advance at Corbera in the same way and retreated at night to the Ebro River. About two a.m., the morning of April third, twenty Mac-Paps got into a truck with orders to go about five miles up the road to observe the enemy from a high ridge. Nick Myers and myself were the only ones from Company 3.

Ten a.m. found us coming down. The enemy were coming alright, and with plenty of tanks. We went to where Bert Hill of Saskatoon had been guarding the truck. Guarding at night alone, not knowing where the enemy were, took plenty of guts. If that truck had not been waiting for us ... well, twenty more men would have died.

We drove back, reported our findings and were ordered to the bridge at Mora d'Ebro where we were the last to cross the river. By now, the government had managed to get most of its supplies across the Ebro into Republican territory. Ten minutes later, the bridge was blown sky high. The fascist drive had been halted—for now.[61]

My small wounds were beginning to bother me: a foot injury when the truck overturned, the burn to my hand when I grabbed the hot barrel, and shrapnel in my leg and back when Stanley Henderson was killed, and I spent ten days in a nice clean hospital, resting and getting fixed up.

Chapter 12
SPECIAL TRAINING

AFTER A FEW DAYS of being hospitalized and resting, I received orders to report to 5th Army headquarters. I was not given the order officially. I was just told to go to the hospital's office where a jeep had been sent for me.[62] [63]

When I arrived at headquarters, my fingerprints were taken and my military book checked—name, number, rank—to make sure I was the right soldier, though I was pretty certain no other person fighting with the government forces had the same name. For one thing, my name would be hard to pronounce in Spanish, the double g's in Higgins, and the "J" in James would be silent.[64]

Before leaving, I produced my identification book again and was given orders to hand to the commanding officer in charge of the operation where I was going—an officer training unit in the mountains—and was to destroy them if there was any chance of being captured. I cannot remember the name of the village, but part of the area we would be travelling through was behind enemy lines where small units of well-armed troops were watching and guarding most of the roads.

My driver, Tom, and I both had side arms, and there was a light machine gun in the jeep in case we needed it. Most of the trip was driven on little more than mule trails that twisted and turned in the mountains. The first time Tom travelled the trail, he had been with two officers and a guide who knew the mountain paths. He had made notes of what to look for at branches in the path and by now was familiar with most of the landmarks, having travelled it a few times.

For somebody who had just been released from hospital, it was unnerving. To make matters worse, an enemy plane came down to strafe us. Tom, who was English and not more than 5'2" (I was 5'7" at the time), let go with, "the bloody, blooming bastards!" as he drove off the trail into cover, almost hitting a tree. We moved away to hide, and the plane came down close to shoot a few more rounds. Tom sounded off with more choice words while we pushed and shoved to get the jeep back on the trail.

We were able to talk more freely when we started up again. Tom told me he had enlisted in England, and when he had reached Spain was sent to a truck pool, a place where cars and army vehicles were kept in repair. Though he had driven ambulances and truckloads of ammo close to the front, this was the first time he had encountered bullets hitting the ground around him.

We had not travelled far when we came across a dead mule and a badly wounded peasant. As we lifted the man into the back of the jeep, I asked Tom if there was a doctor where we were going. He was not sure, though on his last trip to the village, he had a notion that one of the three officers he was driving could have been an army doctor. I sat in the back with the man and did my best to stem his bleeding, using supplies from the first-aid kit.

Within an hour, we entered a small village of about fifty families. A clear stream ran through it, and it seemed well-hidden from the air. There was nothing apart from the villagers' two-room homes and a large stone building guarded by a comrade with an automatic weapon. We stopped at the entrance, and after turning over my order papers, were met by three officers, one of whom I knew.

A doctor showed up immediately. At first, upon seeing my bloody hands and uniform streaked with blood, he thought I was injured, He checked the wounded man and found him close to death. He was taken inside on a stretcher where the doctor removed three bullets. Two of the villagers gave their blood, but he died within three hours and the next morning was buried in the wooded area that surrounded the hamlet.

The packs that had been on the mule contained food for the villagers from the government forces to thank them for their information about enemy movements. Villagers aided the Republicans in many ways. They did not fight back when Franco's forces searched their hamlets, but they did send runners up and down trails to warn others. Information about the enemy would eventually end up with a government force somewhere in the foothills. Later, Tom drove away with three men to skin and quarter the dead mule. I was not surprised the next day to see meat in our stew.

Although the village was in an isolated place in the mountains, and had no military value, it was bombed by a single plane on the sixth day I was there. This time I received a present; a piece of shrapnel in my left wrist. It was immediately looked after by the doctor, who cut into the wound. In removing the fragment, he nicked the vein. My arm was bleeding in spurts, so it was bound tightly below the elbow and he closed the cut with a couple of stitches.

Part of our training was about crossing the Ebro River at night, but mainly it consisted of how to use the modern weapons that had been captured from the Hitler and Mussolini forces, including artillery, machine-guns, and light anti-aircraft guns, the latter named 'pom-poms' as they fired a half-inch shell every second. To say the fascists had superior air power was to put it mildly, since the government had such a small air force that it might as well have been non-existent in the battle zones.

After our training, we were sent back to our battalions with sealed orders. I gave mine to Mac-Pap Commander Cecil-Smith—only he was to know I was now under orders of the 5th Army Corps.[65] [66] [67] He suggested I move into headquarters, but I told him I had verbal orders to keep with the rank and file and that those of us who took the training were not to be promoted for security reasons.[68] [69]

Before this, Captain Medina had known where I was at any given time and received his orders regarding my movements from brigade headquarters. After I received special training, both Captain Medina and Captain Brage gave me orders when a machine-gun was needed.[70] [71] [72]

I had the rank of sergeant at the time, although I would only pin the "stripes" on if top brass came to inspect the unit. It was a very small cloth badge that I would attach to my beret. Very few knew what it was unless they were battalion ranking officers or higher. All of us who took part in that special training had them.

I met up with one later when I was ordered to take my units to aid his company. They were in a tough situation without machine guns; I do not know where. In fact, I did not know where I was most of the time I was in Spain.

I WAS USUALLY TOO busy fighting to have much time for fun, other than joking with my comrades, but there was one time I had a good chuckle. It was May 1938, when our brigade was at rest. Three of us were selected to represent our company at a fiesta, and my buddies and I got into a winery. One was a young Spanish machine gunner named José Díaz.[73][74]

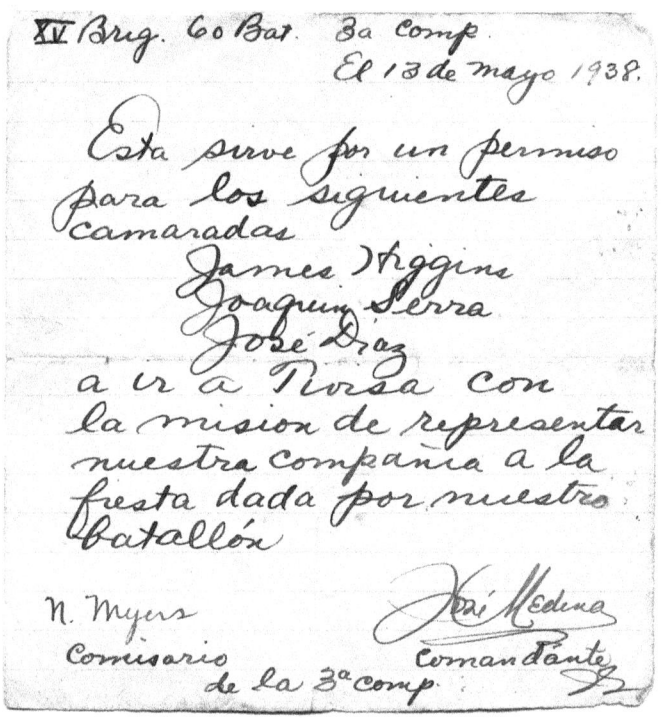

Pass dated May 13, 1938, for Jim Higgins, José Díaz, and Joaquín Serra, to attend a fiesta on behalf of Company 3 (the machine-gun company) of the Mac-Paps. Signed by José Medina (commander) and Nick Myers (commissar of company 3a of the Mac-Paps). Díaz's full name was José Díaz Artacho.

José had been assigned to be my interpreter and assist with training Spanish troops. Few volunteers were arriving now, and their spots in the International Brigades, and in the Spanish Army, were filled with younger and younger Spanish men. José was invaluable to me. We had a special bond, and I made sure any requests for him to be transferred to other units were turned down by the 5th Army Corps. He was with me until I was sent back to Canada.

On our return from the fiesta, I got picked up by Spanish troops and was taken before Captain Medina. Something had to be done about the charges against me, so Medina, who had been in a lot of battles with me, gave me the "punishment" of sweeping out headquarters. As I leaned on my broom, I saw the rest of the battalion going by on a twenty-mile route march with full pack.[75]

This was also the period when I had an amusing encounter with Red Walsh. I first met Red in British Columbia at the start of the On-to-Ottawa trek, where I knew him as an able leader. In the rear, Red had a rank equal to commander of the company, but in the battle zone, his rank could sometimes be that of the leader if the officer in charge was killed or wounded.

Now, during this period of rest for the brigade, he was commissar of the Mac-Pap Number 2 Company and well-respected by all. Each company in our battalion had a political commissar whose responsibility it was to make sure we had food, smokes, ammunition, and other supplies to keep our morale up. We could depend on Red for food that was more to our liking; the Spanish diet was cooked heavily in olive oil with ingredients like chick peas and mule meat that were not palatable to us Canadians.

The Mac-Paps were resting in a valley, and Red had been sent out to get some meat. He asked me and four Spanish comrades to go with him. He had been trying to get a land owner to sell him some goats, which we preferred over mule. "The bastard has about a hundred of the animals, and he will not sell any, regardless of what we offer." By the time I went along, the farmer had refused an offer of three times the market value for a few of his goats.

We could have confiscated the goats, but we tried to avoid that kind of thing because we needed the support of the local people. Also, we knew that some of the richer people were helping the enemy and could be part of a spy network for Franco's nationalist forces. We had been ordered not to bother likely nationalist supporters unless they were caught in the act of informing the other side of our movements. With his large goat herd, that could be the case with this farmer.

Red had permission to use a truck and driver, and we went to the land-owner's place that night to bargain with him one last time. We parked the truck close to the herd and sent the Spanish comrades in to try to make a deal. They returned, saying that the owner refused to sell at any cost. Red sent two of them back with a fistful of money to give to the owner while we loaded five goats onto the truck. We delivered the animals to the cooks and ate very well the next few days, though Red did get into trouble and had to defend himself against a charge.

Three days later, it was back to the battlefield. I was ordered to take the special machine-gun units to help a Spanish battalion trying to hold off an enemy attack. They had already lost about half their men. It was here that I first fought with José Díaz.[76]

Chapter 13
ENEMY SPIES[77]

WE WERE ENTRENCHED BEFORE the last important battle of the war. It was July 1938, and I was with the Mackenzie-Papineau Battalion, having been brought back from special assignment.[78]

The Mac-Paps along with other battalions were scattered over a large area about ten miles from the Ebro River. The comrades were still at rest but also secretly training for a large-scale offensive meant to keep Franco's troops from crossing the Ebro River into what was left of Republican Spain.

I had been chosen to assume responsibility for a training mission with the machine-gun company. We were in a deep valley not far from where the Mac-Paps were camped, but very few other comrades knew about it. We slept in caves we had dug into the sides and trained for a week in a clearing, about thirty yards wide and three hundred yards long, where my units learnt how to use captured enemy weapons.

On the third day, all leaves were cancelled, and we practiced dry runs for crossing the Ebro River at night. Anti-aircraft guns were stationed some distance away to keep an eye out for enemy observation planes. When our pom-poms started firing—the ones we had captured—we ran to the caves and stayed put. There were over three hundred comrades in the camp, and not once were we bombed.

Many in the Mac-Paps were young Spaniards, including my machine-gun units, because we had no more reinforcements coming from Canada. I was concerned about how these boys would react when the going got tough. By now, José Díaz had picked up quite a bit of English, and I asked him what they thought of a stranger to their country leading them.

He put my mind at rest when he said they trusted me, because I admitted I felt fear during battle. I had told them that it was nothing to be ashamed of but not to let fear be their master and not to let their fellow soldiers notice. I told them to focus on overcoming the obstacle, and in that way, their fear would diminish. José said they respected me because I had spoken to them in this way; if I had been overbearing and threatening, he thought they would not have taken to me.

I taught them how to use the captured weapons and took them out with light Bren and Czech machine guns with a round of ammo for each gun. That would be eighty to ninety bullets. José was a great help in explaining things. Before we crossed the Ebro River, ten Spanish youngsters who knew how to handle the weapons. They would replace experienced Mac-Pap gunners killed in the action to come.

At the appointed time, we made our trek to the bank of the Ebro in the dark. This was one time we had two heavy Maxims, with shields and wheels, and other light machine-guns. These were loaded onto the truck, which drove slowly (without lights) so those who were walking could keep up. I was on the truck because my next special assignment was to be in charge of machine-gun squads that, most of the time, would be behind enemy lines.[79][80]

It was growing light when we reached trenches dug for us by a Spanish labour battalion. Labour battalions were made up of those who had a tendency to get drunk and cause trouble. Instead of a rifle, they got a pick and shovel.

The fortifications were well-camouflaged, with communication tunnels to the rear. Small boats for our use were hidden in the tree-lined river bank. There was to be no firing across the river, regardless of movement.

Unfortunately, one of our men decided to test a captured Italian gun and fired off a few shots. It was a foolish thing to do because it could alert the enemy to our position. I had to report him, though I mentioned it was an enemy gun he was unfamiliar with. Of course, he still received a bawling out from battalion headquarters.

THE SPY INCIDENT HAPPENED just before we crossed the Ebro. Spies were everywhere, even behind enemy lines, and when the enemy retreated, they would leave spies in our territory with "papers" and Republican money. It was hard for either side to detect spies because we were moving around so much.

I had been watching the opposite side of the river for enemy movements but had not seen anything unusual. On the second morning, I was instructed to check a farmhouse about half a mile to the right on our side of the river and told to concentrate on a clothesline that had been changed by a man in civilian clothes at least five times the day before.

We could see it clearly through field glasses. Within an hour, a man came out of the house and rearranged the garments. I sketched the two arrangements, showing colour and shape. The same thing happened in another two hours. After my second report back to the command post, I received an order to bring the occupants in for questioning.

José Díaz picked two Canadians and two young Spanish men who had been with us during the machine-gun training before we moved to the Ebro position. I gave instructions on how to proceed—José interpreted to the Spanish lads—and we moved about six yards apart under cover of the woods, myself in the lead and José in the rear.

We reached the back of the building, and leaving the other four in the cover, José and I approached a door that fronted on the river. We knocked. Nobody answered, but we could hear movement and voices inside. We pounded on the door with our weapons and ordered the occupants to open up.

The door was opened by a frightened-looking woman. Another was standing behind her. The two women spoke quietly to José, and he motioned for all four of us to go outside. José whispered to me that there were two armed men in the cellar and that the women were wives of comrades in a Spanish battalion. I sent José back to the woods with the women and asked him to bring two of our comrades back with him. The other two were to take the women to the command post.

Four of us entered the house and surrounded the entrance to the cellar. We threw the trap door open and ordered the occupants up. The threat of a hand grenade being thrown down brought up two men.

One was taken outside while José and I questioned the other. He told us he belonged to a Spanish battalion stationed in the rear. This would be checked when we turned them over to our command. When we asked why they were in civilian clothing, he said their commander had ordered them to dress that way. José and I both knew this was phoney.

I held my gun on the prisoner while José went out to get a flashlight from one of the details. Just then, Red Walsh arrived. This time it was more serious than making off with a few goats.

Red suggested we check the house before searching the cellar. Nothing was found, so the prisoner was ordered below. I admit I had butterflies in my guts as I followed him down. As expected, the cellar was booby-trapped—I found a trip wire that could have triggered two grenades. They also had three Italian rifles. I was relieved when I came up with no trouble.

It was dusk by this time, and Red suggested that the clothes on the line be changed. The women had told us there were other men coming and going, so we left two comrades in the building to apprehend anyone who came during the night, while we took the two prisoners back to the command post. The next morning, two other prisoners wearing civilian clothes were brought in.

That night, Red told me the prisoners admitted the women were hostages, and that they had been sending signals to the enemy. This was enough to be shot by a firing squad. I knew if the prisoners had been wearing some kind of military uniform, they would not have been killed. I also knew that many lives on our side were saved during the next few days because of their capture.

When Red was telling me what happened to the men, he was wearing boots that I was fairly certain one of them had been wearing. When I asked how he got them, Red replied that the past owner would not be needing them. I looked at my own boots and hoped I would get a change before they fell off my feet. It was the last time I saw Red, though I know he made it home to Canada.

MEANWHILE, SMALL ARMS AND mortar fire could be heard on our distant right flank. The leaders knew that meant the enemy was being drawn away from our area by an engagement a few miles away. This kept up all day, and we knew the time was close when we would make our move that night.

Other battalions were on our flanks: British, American, German (men who had escaped from Nazi Germany), and two Spanish battalions in reserve. It is hard to believe that so many troops had been able to assemble without enemy spotter planes noticing something.

We crossed the Ebro River without incident the night of July 25, 1938 and were five miles into enemy territory before we met any opposition worth mentioning. It was then that bombing and shelling started, and things got rough as we tried to keep in touch with our command post for orders. During the night of the twenty-sixth, the enemy rushed up troops and tanks.

We were a small unit by then and had our machine guns covering a road along which the enemy was trying to move troops to better positions. Besides the riflemen, there were five more of our machine guns scattered in the cover.

Everything and anything happened from then on. Units lost track of their companies and battalions were scattered all over "hell's half acre." There *was* no front. One day, towns and villages were invaded by one side in the fight, and the next, the other side would surround it.

In the midst of the chaos, we learnt that news media all over the world reported that we had performed a miracle by crossing the Ebro and attacking superior forces. But to us, it was clear the enemy's superior weapons and manpower were taking their toll.

Today, I think of it as the final jerk that an animal gives before death.

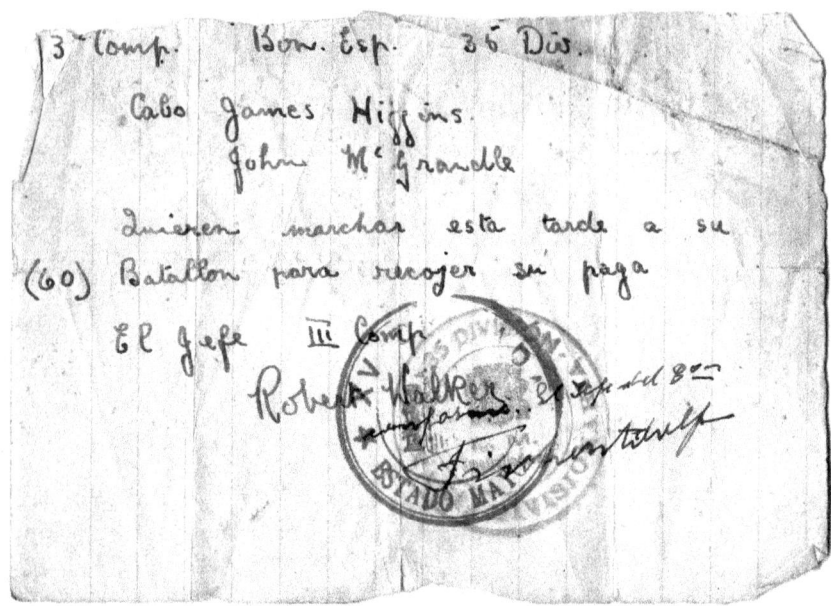

Higgins was with the Mac-Paps in July 1938, before crossing the Ebro, but fought with the 35th Division in August and September. This undated pass from the 35th Division, for James Higgins and John McGrandle to collect their July pay from the Mac-Paps, was likely issued in August.

Chapter 14
THE BATTLE OF THE EBRO[81]

TWO DAYS LATER, JOSÉ Díaz and I were in the hilltop town of Corbera, helping civilians bombed by Franco's planes. It was one of the many towns and villages that I passed through or stayed in for a short time. We had been sent into the town to search for victims but found most of the people had spread to the outskirts where there would be less chance of being bombed.

We were just leaving when a bomb hit a water tank. Suddenly, José noticed a body being swept down the steep hill flooded by water from the burst tank. I took off my coat, gave José my pistol and three hand grenades, and told him to make sure the machine gun was guarded.

The water was only two feet deep, but it had a strong current. I waded in and managed to grab the victim, a boy of about twelve, as he sped by. Within a minute, I pulled him close to the edge. He could not walk because of injuries caused by rocks and debris. I carried him on my back through a vineyard to a first-aid station in a winery, lying low when bombers flew overhead.

I stepped carefully along the slippery edge of the winery's sludge tanks to deliver him. The boy was given first aid and sent to a hospital in the rear. I was given a blanket while my bloody clothes were washed and dried.

While I was carrying the boy, I tried to tell him (in the best Spanish I could muster) that I was Canadian and that my name was Jim. I did not have to struggle to save the boy. It was easy for me to rescue him. Anyway, I doubt the lad survived.[82] [83]

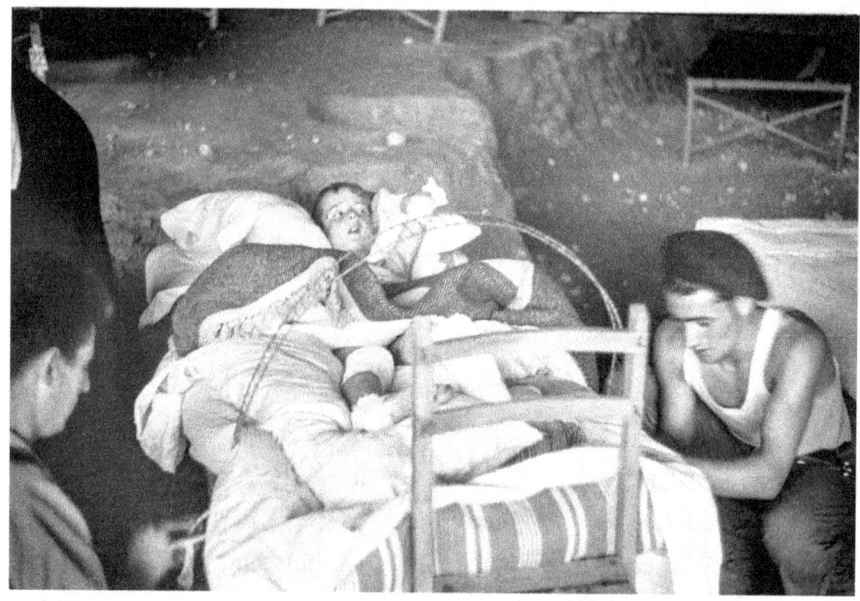

The "lad" did survive, but Higgins did not find out until forty years later when Manuel Alvarez finally tracked him down to thank him. It took another forty years for Alvarez to be identified in this long-lost picture taken by Alec Wainman in the cave hospital near La Bisbal de Falset, Terres de l'Ebre, Spain in early August 1938. Copyright The Estate of Alexander Wheeler Wainman, John Alexander Wainman (Serge Alternes).[84]

WE DID NOT STAY long in that town as I had been ordered to take the gun to help a Spanish company that needed cover while they moved to a stronger position.[85] A runner took us to the unit, and we reported to their command post. José translated, and we learnt that they were in a tight spot, unable to move from their shallow trenches which were under machine-gun fire. Through my field glasses, I could see that two enemy machine guns had them pinned down. Noting where the guns were, I asked the officer to let me have two of his men.

At dusk, we set our gun to cover the enemy guns. I could not tie the gun down and cover both, but we had figured the range and direction of one of their guns, and as the trapped Spanish company moved back, we started firing. Because of the dark, we could only aim at the enemy flashes, so we focussed on knowing that they had less cover than ourselves. José fired bursts of six or seven at a time until I told him to elevate a fraction.

Within three minutes, the enemy gun we were shooting at stopped firing. From the sound, I knew they did not have a water-cooled weapon, as we had, and that their steady firing had heated the barrel till it jammed—that or we had been lucky and hit the target.

Bullets from the second enemy gun were getting too close, and one of our ammo carriers was wounded. I moved our gun about thirty yards to the left. We had all the ammo we needed, but the gun was getting hot. I asked José and the other comrade to piss into a large can, and I helped by letting the excess water out of my system. I then drained the can into the gun to cool it down.

The first enemy gun remained silent, so we knew our fire had caused trouble. The second gun was still blasting away in the direction of our first position. Two more boys from the Spanish unit had been sent in with rifles to divert the enemy from our gun's location.

José put them at ease and placed them about twenty yards away. He told me they were the best marksmen in the unit. They were to take careful aim in the direction of the gun flashes and lay down in the trench when the enemy started spraying their area.

By now our gun had cooled down, and it was time for us to open up. We did not spare the ammunition and kept a steady fire towards the second gun. Within five minutes, it had been silenced. Our attempt to fool them had succeeded. Shortly after, José was told that what was left of the Spanish company was entrenched, and we were to retire and await further orders.

For the next few days, our gun was sent to help in similar actions. At times, I had to call on other machine-gun squads to help. I lost five comrades, three killed and two wounded.

Later, my outfit was ordered to secure a village. A company of Mac-Paps had driven the Franco forces out, and we were to make sure that none of the enemy remained. I set up our two light machine guns—they were Czech—to cover two streets that came together in the shape of a "V."

We set up our guns where the streets converged. One gun was at ground level, and the other on the second storey of a house where it could cover both areas. Sixteen comrades with rifles moved slowly, about five yards apart, on each side of each street. Each comrade's mission was to watch the roofs and upper windows of the houses on the opposite side.

Shots rang out from one of the comrades across the street and an enemy soldier smashed to the road near me. The hand grenade he had thrown just as he was shot exploded. The comrade behind me got it in the face, but I was wearing a heavy khaki coat, and though I got a few small pieces of shrapnel in my back, they did not go deep so I did not report the injury.[86]

A FEW DAYS LATER, I was almost shot by a communist officer. It was while I was on guard duty, one of the longest six hours I have experienced. I could not smoke—I did not have any tobacco—and could not take a walk because I would have had to leave my post and expose myself. Once in a while, I checked my watch. Just after four a.m., I heard someone approaching.

Keeping in the shadow, I waited. A flashlight flicked on and lit up part of the spot where I was crouching. Then a voice ordered me to come out in the open. I knew him as a parade-ground soldier who had never been in any real fight action. I told him to put the flashlight out and keep his hand away from the gun in his strapped-down holster.

He did what I ordered, and I exposed myself near the entrance to the street with the safety latch off my rifle. He then ordered me to give him the weapon so he could check to see if it was in working order. I refused and told him to put his hands up and then shouted for the officer who had placed me at the post, giving the post number.

In a few seconds, the officer arrived with a tommy gun at the ready. He was backed up by another comrade holding a pistol. I explained what had happened. The officer who had accosted me was relieved of his weapon and taken away, but not before he told me I would be taken before the commander of the unit in the morning.

At six a.m., the guard was changed, and I went to the guard house and slept with my boots on until I was awakened and taken to the *Estado Mayor*—the command post. Captain Medina questioned me regarding the incident and told me not to worry; I had done the correct thing. He dismissed me without further comment.[87]

IT HAD NOW BEEN ten days since I received the shrapnel wound, and it had infected my back. I was sent to a hospital near Barcelona and examined by a doctor.[88] [89] [90] After a day of luxury, having a real bed with clean (albeit blood-stained) sheets and eating well—eggs, fresh vegetables, stew made with real beef, and powdered milk that tasted fresh and wonderful—the doctor went to work.

I received a needle in the hip and a shot of rye. With no chloroform, all I could do was hold onto something and grit my teeth as the doctor removed the shrapnel. He then daubed the wounds with something that smarted like hell, but the grub and bed more than made up for the pain.

On the third day, I was taken to a rehabilitation centre in a convent. It was a four-sided stone building with a single entrance that led to an inner courtyard. In the middle was a statue and fountain that did not work. Each of the ground level rooms had four to ten cots and there were always six nurses and a doctor on duty.

There was a veranda all around the upper storey of the building. Here, there were single rooms about six feet wide and eight feet long—something like prison cells. These, I was told, were where the nuns had lived. I was also told tales—true or false, at that point I had no way to verify—that priests were allowed to visit the nuns in these cells to listen to their "confessions."

Apparently, some priests visited certain nuns quite often, and sometimes a birth was the result. The pregnancy would go unnoticed because of the habits the nuns wore. To hide the births, the babies were smothered and gotten rid of.

I was assigned to a room with four cots and became friendly with Joe, an American whose right arm had been disabled when an explosive bullet hit him in the shoulder. On the second day, Joe told me I could get an overnight pass for Barcelona. The pass was needed to show anyone wearing a uniform or to patrols who spot-checked civilians.

Three of us got passes with the official stamp, signed by the major at the rehabilitation centre. The third comrade was an Irishman named Paddy. He had been hospitalized for some time with a wound in the neck and was waiting to be sent home. His vocal cords had been affected, and he could barely make himself understood.

We bummed a ride with an ambulance driver who went out of his way to take us to the Majestic Hotel. He refused our offer of a couple of hundred pesetas, so we left it on the seat. Joe could communicate better in Spanish, and in no time, we had picked up two girls who were sipping wine at a sidewalk cafe. We had two girls and three guys, so I offered to pick up a girl for myself.

One of the girls mentioned that she had a sister but was not sure if she would agree. Opening my packsack, I brought out a bar of laundry soap, cut off three inches, and gave it to the girl. Laundry soap was worth something, and she went home to get her sister, Anita. I was glad Paddy and Joe were with the other girls, because Anita could speak English.

The six of us went to a movie. We presented our passes, and the girls got in free. When we went back to the hotel, we were stopped twice by patrols but had no problem when we showed our passes. The second time we were stopped, Anita interpreted to the cabo in charge. She told him that I had been at the front for nine months, and it was the first time I had been with a woman. The soldiers addressed the other two girls by their first names, but Anita was unknown to them.

We had a large room with two beds in the bigger part and another behind a partition. I had a notion that the partitioned area was probably used by correspondents, because there was a desk. The windows were taped and covered, and the only light was behind the partition where my bed was.

Anita, now my bed companion, spoke about her upbringing. She confirmed the stories I had heard about pregnant nuns and told me she had been forced to enter a convent by her family and the all-powerful church. There, she had a baby, fathered by a priest, who was taken away as soon as it was born. She did not know what happened to it and was very bitter.

She also told me stories that had been passed down through generations. Like other poor families, they had been permeated with the Catholic faith. At least one child in each family was encouraged to enter a convent or religious order. It was often the youngest girls, because their parents could not afford any more marriage dowries.

Even the rich had to release their daughters to the church, but there was a difference: They went to convents for those of noble birth that were much more comfortable. "Noble" meant they had fathers who had either bought their titles or been granted a knighthood by the former king as a reward for military service. The daughters of the poor existed in cells identical to the ones on the second floor at the rehabilitation centre.

That night, and the next day, I took Anita to two meals, and we talked a lot until my pass required me to return to the rehab facility. I learnt a lot but was a complete flop sexually and felt I had to apologize. I think—I know—she felt sorry for me.

AT THE TIME OF my hospital stay, the international volunteers had been recalled and their battalions disbanded, but as far as I was concerned, the defensive fighting was long from over.[91] Before the end of the war, the Army Corps wisely destroyed the material that could be used to pinpoint any international who was likely to be captured or left behind in Spain.

José Díaz and I were together many months. Twice, officers wanted to take him away, and I had to go to the top brass to keep him. He was away from me only once; a week when he was hospitalized with a flesh wound in his thigh.

It was a bitter day in the third week of January 1939, when the commander of the Spanish company I was fighting with told José to inform me that a jeep had been sent to take me to the village where the Mac-Paps were gathered to leave Spain. I think I was the last Mac-Pap in a Spanish unit.[92] José was the one to deliver the message, because no one else in the company spoke English.

If that young Spaniard is still alive today, he will remember the tears that came to my eyes as we embraced and said goodbye. I had seen comrades and civilians wounded and killed, but only felt hatred for the enemy, no tears. My parting from José was different. I felt that I had lost a part of my life. I am still emotional about it today.

My last words to him were that, when Franco took over, not to admit he had fought with the international volunteers. I hoped it might save him from a concentration camp.[93] [94] [95] [96] [97] [98]

Don (1) *Willy Glasser Capitan Medico, Director Clinica Militar n° 17*

CERTIFICO: Que don (2) ~~Higgins James~~

Higgins James

de 31 años de edad, clasificado (3) *Inform*

presta sus servicios en concepto de (4)

en (5) *Clinica Militar No 17*

desde (6) *el dia 1°.X.38*

por ~~haber~~ sido destinado por orden de

Y para que conste, expido el presente certificado-salvoconducto, que tendrá validez hasta el día *15-XI-38*

en *Vich* a (de *noviembre*

de

(Sello)   (Firma)

(1) Cargo de quien expide el documento.
(2) Nombre, apellidos y graduación.
(3) Útil, apto servicios auxiliares, pendiente de revisión, inútil, etc.
(4) Cometido concreto.
(5) Unidad, Cuerpo o Dependencia.
(6) Fecha que corresponda.

Huellas dactilares del interesado

Salvoconducto *(Safe Conduct Pass) issued to Higgins at Clinica Militar 17 on November 1, 1938, signed by Captain Willy Glasser. It is valid until November 15. Why two weeks? And why the fingerprints? After all, he wasn't finger-printed for the pass to go into Barcelona from the rehab facility, nor for his other two passes that survive. An official stamp would seem sufficient for travel in the relatively safe territory where he was north of Barcelona. Interestingly, Higgins made a point of being fingerprinted in April before being taken to the secluded place in the mountains where he received special training for the Ebro Offensive. Was this for something secret as well? Random notes found in his papers offer tantalizing but unverified clues, "Nov 15. I was not there for the final great farewell parade. I was still fighting. Catalonia Nov Dec 1938," and "Last activities in Spain. Blowing up bridge (Ebro)."[99] Also headquarters (Albacete) with IB documents and passports. Last days in Spain."[100 101 102]*

105

Ration card for Clinica Militar 17 showing Higgins there from December 1-10, 1938. His replica Carnet Militar, *containing misinformation about his service, was probably made there since it is dated December 3, 1938.*

Higgins's Filiacion (affiliation form), dated January 25, 1939, was completed in the nick of time. The next day, as Franco was bombing and capturing nearby Barcelona, most Mac-Paps were leaving Spain on a sealed train across France. Once in England, they travelled to Liverpool and boarded the Duchess of Richmond.

When Jim Higgins crossed the Pyrenees into Spain, he gazed in awe at the calm Mediterranean sparkling in the sun, but later reflected, "A wealth of experience, of love and hate, passed between that first glimpse and the last." His last view would have been of thousands of desperate refugees escaping over the border into France. In this photo, taken at the end of fifteen months in Spain, his face says it all.

Chapter 15
HEROES TO THE PEOPLE

A GROUP OF FIFTY-NINE of us returning Mac-Paps disembarked from the *Duchess of Richmond* at Halifax and boarded a special train to Toronto. It was Friday, February 3, 1939. With us was Edward Cecil-Smith, our battalion commander. As our train left, the main group of about two hundred vets was disembarking and boarding a bigger train.

During our voyage, I had been bunked in the cabin across from Cecil-Smith and acting as political commissar. Part of my duty was to be in charge of the canvas where our boys pinned comments and where Cecil-Smith posted cablegrams from our citizen support committee in Canada—the Friends of the Mackenzie-Papineau Battalion in Spain.

Despite the Canadian government having made our actions illegal under the Foreign Enlistment Act, we knew we had broad support from the people of Canada. They had sent us letters, cigarettes, and care packages throughout the war, and they (like us) saw the danger of fascism long before the federal government finally had to admit that Hitler was a threat.

We knew from the cablegrams that there would be a citizen welcome for us in Toronto. Still, when we arrived at Union Station, it was almost overwhelming. A huge mass of people greeted us, estimated by news reports to be ten thousand. Hundreds spilled out onto Front Street, because there was not enough room in the station.[103]

Our advance group arrived a few hours before the larger group on the later train, so we knew the boys' friends and relatives had been waiting for hours. The other vets finally arrived, and we marched in formation behind our banners in a roped-off area to the cheers of the crowd.

The ropes were removed, and it was a touching scene as families met their sons. I was saddened by those who did not find their loved ones but was happy to see eyes light up when I passed along news of those I knew were alive.

An hour or so later, a couple came up to me and asked if I had a place to go. I told them I did not, and they took me to their home where I stayed for

> Ballentine Board on ship returning to Canada.
> Original Feb 1939
>
> Spain overrun by Fascism will present France and Britain with a major problem. If they wish to avoid it they must at once abolish the not only wicked but stupid policy of embargo against the Spanish government.
>
> We, as returning ex-members of the International Brigades, will certainly do all we can to line Canada up with the United States in opposition to the embargo.
>
> The embargo lifted, Spain will be able to better defend world democracy. The next step after that must be to force the withdrawal of all foreign troops from Spain and the terrible threat of world war will disappear, at least for the time being.
>
> E. Cecil Smith.

Jim Higgins was commissar to Commander Edward Cecil-Smith on the ship home, which included looking after the bulletin board. Before the Mac-Paps disembarked, Higgins removed this message printed by Cecil-Smith about the "terrible threat of a world war" if the West's embargo on Spain was not lifted. (Higgins later wrote across the top.) Within months, Hitler invaded Poland on September 1, 1939. Two days after that, France and Britain declared war on Germany, launching World War II. Countries that refused to help Spain fight fascism were finally forced to recognize Hitler for what he was.

The Mac-Paps arrived at Union Station on February 4, 1939. Commander Edward Cecil-Smith, wearing wire-rimmed glasses, is to the right of the second flag. Higgins, wearing a fedora, circled his own head. The photo is in Higgins's copy of The Mackenzie-Papineau Battalion.[104]

two weeks. Their names were Phil and Mae Dawes, and they became lifelong friends, though I did not see much of them at that time. I was kept busy with plans for a rally on February sixth at Massey Hall and, after, with meetings with sympathizers.

On the evening of February fifth, about one hundred vets and their supporters marched to a church service, myself among them. As the church became filled to overflowing, many supporters had to be turned away. The thrust of the sermon, delivered by Reverend R. H. Thomas, National Chairman of our Rehabilitation Fund, concerned the medical and housing needs of the vets.[105]

The Massey Hall rally was the next morning. The rehearsal lasted an hour, and I then went to get a haircut and something to eat before contacting other vets to ensure they had transportation. An hour before the public arrived, I helped direct the vets to their places on the stage.

Phil and Mae Dawes went to Union Station to cheer the Mac-Paps as heroes, along with 10,000 other Canadians. The Daweses gave Jim a place of refuge and became lifelong friends. Jim's children called them "Aunt" and "Uncle" and in 2010 their son, Cameron, married Jim's daughter, Barbara.

Massey Hall had been rented to us at a much-reduced fee, partly through the impressive connections of the Friends of the Mackenzie-Papineau Battalion; rabbis, clergymen, the Dean of Chichester, the Toronto mayor and aldermen, other elected officials from provincial and federal governments, and writers Ernest Hemingway, Upton Sinclair, H. G. Wells, and J. B. S. Haldane. The list also included well-known doctors and academics.

The curtain went up at Massey Hall, and the applause became a standing ovation with a roar that deafened the ears. The chairman was finally able to call the people to order, and the bugle sounded the Last Post for our comrades who died in Spain.

During the next several days, I was invited to the homes of those who supported our fight against Hitler and Mussolini—people as sure as we were that Spain's battlegrounds had been used as a test for Nazi and fascist weapons to be used in a war against the unprepared democracies of Europe.

One of those invitations was from Reverend Thomas, who wanted me to help him with the rehabilitation campaign in the western provinces. It involved organizing local committees to raise funds for the wounded as well as visiting the parents of those who were killed. I told him I was not sure I could handle the job.

Later, I was invited by the president of a local union to attend a meeting. It was not until I saw members from other unions in the sign-in book that I realized it was a meeting of the Toronto Labour Council. I was steered to the front and given a seat.

The place was packed, with people left outside. There was an empty chair beside the president, and during the clapping at my introduction, I tried to figure who it was for. I was still mystified when there was a commotion at the door and the guard came up and spoke to the chairman. He went to the door and requested those who jammed it to clear a passage to let the guest in.

It was the Reverend Thomas. He was escorted to the empty seat and apologized for being late. He explained that he had been visiting the family of a worker who had been killed in a workplace accident and mentioned the need for laws to enforce safety standards and of the need for workers to be active in their unions.

Then he got down to his main purpose, addressing the needs of the veterans and asking for the support of the unions. It also became apparent why I was there. It was the push I needed. I agreed to go west.

I was given three contacts in Saskatoon where I would be based: the labour council secretary, the president of a local railroad union, and the minister of St. Andrews Presbyterian Church, the Reverend W. G. Brown.

I also had information about the vets, their addresses so I could get aid to them, and if I was visiting a bereaved family, where they had been killed or gone missing in battle. I was given train fare and twenty-five dollars. For further funds, I would receive money from local committees.

During the journey, I continued to have misgivings about whether the mission was more than I could handle. I reread the letter of introduction and took out my ID card, stamped and signed by two top members of the "Friends" head office committee. That was when I noticed that both had a printer's union label. Those small emblems took me back to the comradeship and struggles I had experienced in the unions before I left for Spain and helped raise my mood of depression.

Then I thought back to a vet I had visited in a Toronto hospital who had returned to Canada on a stretcher. His face was bandaged and strapped, and he had lost a leg and an arm; he would need hospital care for some time, and later, artificial limbs.

As soon as I entered the hospital ward, he croaked, "Is that you, Jimmie?" He continued with some effort. "I thought you were killed when your squad was sent out that morning at Azuara. That was the day I was pretty near given up for dead."

"I'll always remember that day," I told him. "It was pure hell. I still don't understand how I survived."

I was reminded that this experience was another reason I agreed to go out west to raise funds for my comrades.

I arrived in Saskatoon in late February 1939, expecting to see three people at the train station, only to find a big crowd.[106] I was overcome by the welcome, and as the Reverend Brown addressed the group, I relaxed and realized my earlier misgivings were unfounded.

I covered Winnipeg, Calgary, Edmonton, Lethbridge, Regina, and other smaller prairie towns. I worked with labour councils and local unions, which joined with other groups to set up committees to organize the appeals for money to help with the rehabilitation of the vets. The railway unions were especially helpful in my travels. I was given a card to identify myself to union members in the caboose of any freight train.

The men shared their lunches with me, and even the railroad "bulls" had to go along. The few tough bully types knew not to report the trainmen for breaking the rules. I heard how one of the bulls reported a member for some minor incident. The word was passed around, and whenever he was on one of their freights, they played tricks (like tossing his club out) to make his life miserable.

Early on, I crossed swords with the mayor and city council of Saskatoon, when I appeared before them to ask for permission to hold a tag day to raise funds for the wounded vets.[107] Besides maligning me, they called into question the legitimacy of the Reverend Thomas, our national campaign chairman back in Toronto.[108 109]

This encounter with city officials had been reported in the Saskatoon Star-Phoenix, and if I recall correctly, the news headline was something like, "Spanish Vet Seeks Aid from City Council." However, the article was laced with implied meanings that I was a communist, and cast aspersions against mine and Thomas's integrity. Ironically, the controversy that played out in the press gave the aid committee valuable publicity, and later helped in electing our candidate over the Liberal opponent.[110 111 112 113]

I spent five months raising funds for disabled and hospitalized vets and cannot remember ever buying a meal or paying to sleep. After the experiences I had been through in Spain, I had to adjust my mind to believe this sort of kindness was possible.

I WAS IN REGINA raising funds when I received word from labour-council friends in Saskatoon that they wanted me to organize a federal election campaign for a recently-formed group representing interests and parties on the left. We soon agreed to call it the United Reform Movement.[114 115]

I must explain the political history of the city of Saskatoon. It had never, over the previous twenty plus years, elected any person other than a Liberal as Member of Parliament. The city council and daily newspaper, the *Star-Phoenix*, were strongly tilted to the Liberal Party; even the Royal Canadian Legion executive committee could be included in that bracket, except for the secretary, who was a good friend of mine.

The day after I received the request from the labour council, I travelled back to Saskatoon, via caboose, and let the railroaders know what I was hoping to accomplish. They promised me their union would give us every possible support.

Back in Saskatoon, I asked several organizations to send representatives to a meeting. I had spent time there before the Spanish Civil War and knew members of the ethnic and progressive groups very well.

Three days later, twelve of us gathered in a large living room, including delegates from the Co-operative Commonwealth Federation (CCF), the Communist Party of Canada (CPC), and the Polish and Ukrainian organizations. I was selected to chair the meeting and asked the secretary of a local union to record the session.

I cautioned, "We can win the next federal election only if we have complete unity. We have to bury our differences until the campaign is over. If we remain united, I don't see any reason for us to fail. We must always keep in mind the reason we are here tonight is to unite forces to get our candidate elected.

"As for the candidate, the Reverend W. G. Brown has agreed to consider running, and will give us a firm answer within a day or so. Three of us have had a talk with him and feel he will take the chance, if he's sure that all of your organizations will back him.

"As you all know, bickering and the problem of every group wanting to do their own thing, in the early months, lost the war in Spain before it started. Franco, Hitler, Mussolini, and the church were so united at the outset that they got the jump on the divided forces trying to defend the elected government. So let us all unite behind one goal; to do our utmost to beat the Liberal party."

I got together with four representatives of our group before meeting with Reverend Brown.[116] I mentioned that Brown did not belong to any political party, nor would he accept the nomination if he felt he was being pressured. I reminded them of what they well knew; he had a long history of doing what he could to help society's underdogs.[117]

As anybody who knows me is aware, I am not the most diplomatic person in the world. I communicate in a very direct way that mature people can accept. That is the line I took in dealing with the election committee members.

There was only one person who did not see eye-to-eye with me; a delegate representing the communist party. He wanted the candidate to take a hard line. I was forced to put him down and other members of the committee sided with me.

After the meeting, I had a talk with the secretary of the local communist party and told him to either replace the delegate or tell him to cooperate. Three days later, he had been replaced by a more reasonable person who accepted the will of the majority vote at the meetings.

I was also invited to have a coffee with the two representatives of the Polish and Ukrainian groups. It happened that, besides representing their own organizations, one was a member of the CPC and the other was a CCF member. Each complained that the campaign was not socialistic enough.

I asked each how many card-carrying members they had in their own ethnic organization. The communist admitted that only three out of two hundred members in his group were communist party members. The CCF member said he knew of only ten card-carrying CCF members in his. I asked them if they were not willing at least to vote for some kind of limited change in an area which had long been a stronghold of Liberal politics. Reluctantly, they agreed.

Each committee member was given responsibilities and reported in at weekly meetings.[118] An apolitical writer friend agreed to research and write the campaign pamphlet. Like me, he *was* not—*would* not—be tied down by any political party. A committee of five changed the pamphlet a bit, and I took it to a union printer to have it printed as a four-page campaign flyer, complete with union label.

We were a tight group and had no contact with outside reform parties. It seemed unreal to see the CCF and communist party delegates putting their differences aside. All during the campaign, they worked with the Ukrainian and

Polish organizations in a spirit of sincere cooperation. I wished it could be on a worldwide scale.

The people of Saskatoon elected our candidate, W. G. Brown, and sent him to Ottawa as their Member of Parliament.[119] [120] [121]

Looking back, that campaign committee was the most unified group of people I have ever been associated with in an election. I had trouble believing the trust they had in me to map the way forward but had the satisfaction of knowing that hard work and a united people had been responsible. The odd one hated my guts, though later admitted a grudging respect for me.

WHILE I WAS STILL in Saskatoon, the Second World War erupted. Right away, Canada was looking for volunteers to fight. I tried to sign up but made the mistake of telling recruiters that I had been a machine gunner in Spain. I was told to come back the following week.

When I returned, the colonel said, "We can't take you."

I said, "Why not?"

He said, "You're a security risk." And that was it![122] [123] [124]

It was with regret that I left Saskatoon a few months later. I had made many friends, and even my personal life had been very satisfactory, having a relationship with no strings attached; gratifying after my near zero performance in Spain.

I only left because the RCMP was becoming a little too interested in my past.[125] [126]

The RCMP would have been alerted to Higgins's location as soon as he returned from Spain. (Other vets received similar attention.) Higgins kept this envelope as evidence of RCMP tampering. It had been mailed from Saskatoon in October 1938.

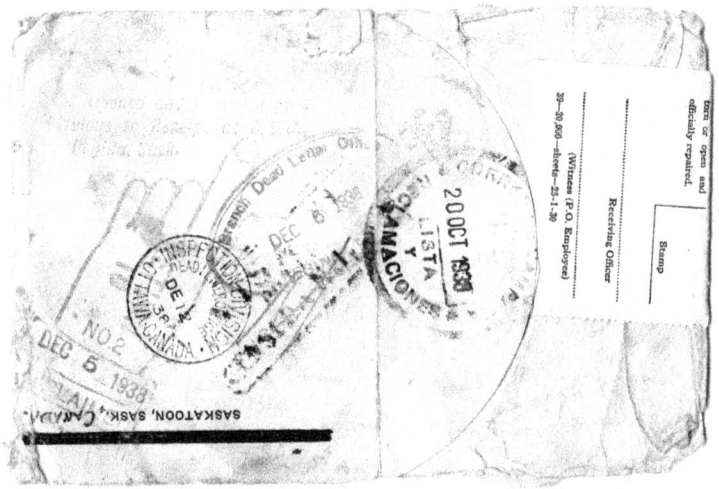

Stamps on the back indicate the letter arrived at the International Brigades mail depot in Barcelona on October 20th, was returned as unclaimed, then opened and resealed at the dead letter office in Regina on December 5th. On December 12th, it was stamped by the "Inspection Division Dead Letter Office" in Ottawa. Only then was the envelope returned to its sender, who gave it to Higgins when he returned to Saskatoon in February 1939.

Chapter 16
OVER THE BORDER ON A BIKE

IT WAS SPRING 1940 when I thought it wise to leave Canada for a short while to escape heat from the RCMP.[127] Besides, I wanted to visit families of a few American vets who had been killed by my side as well as see friends from the Lincoln Battalion in New York.

I left Canada unofficially. I first headed to British Columbia where I bought a bike with a basket attached to the handlebars and a carrier on the rear for a bedroll. I also had a rainproof packsack that contained toiletries and a change of clothes. I picked a border village without any customs agents. After changing my money on the Canadian side I crossed the street and was in the United States. It was quite easy to do.

It took three days of biking to reach the first family. Their son had sent them my name in case he was killed, and they had written to me after he died, while I was still in Spain. I was glad to visit them for a couple of days. They wanted me to stay longer, but I had other families to see. The father drove me about sixty miles east with my bicycle in the back of his pickup truck. I then took a more or less direct route to Ohio with support from kind people along the way.

One who helped was a highway patrol officer who had passed me a few times before I stopped at a roadside diner. The officer came in shortly after and asked me where I was headed. I told him I was going to visit family in New York. During our small talk, he said he could tell I was a "New Yorker" by my accent!

I left the diner and had biked about five miles along the road when a pickup truck stopped. I was invited to put my bike in the back and ride up front with the owner. He took me about forty miles, and I learnt that the cop had asked him to look out for me.

In all, I was on the road for about six months. At night, I usually slept behind a fence in fields along the highway. Sometimes I slept in quarries where stone had been taken out to build the road. Otherwise, I did the same thing I had during the Depression: I would ask at a farm if I could do chores the next day in exchange for a place to sleep in their barn. I was never turned down, though I did very little work.

People were pleased to have a traveller to talk to. We discussed the Depression in Canada, but I mentioned nothing about Spain. They often wanted me to stay longer, but I was impatient to get to Ohio where I visited the family of a man who had died in my unit.

The Ohio family had a corn farm, and I worked there for about two weeks. The father took me to everything that was going on in town and paid my way. He wanted me to stay on when he saw I could drive trucks and tractors, but I said I needed to get to New York to visit other families who had lost their boys. At the end of the two weeks, I sold my bike to the farmer's son and took a bus to New York. It was the fall of 1940.

I was met at the Port Authority bus station by the sister of a boy killed in one of my machine-gun units. She had taken a half day off work, and we went to her home on the lower east side by subway. They were Jewish people, not orthodox. They and other families treated me as though I was one of their own.

Parties were arranged where I met Jewish vets who fought with the Abraham Lincoln Battalion, some of whom were already friends. I decided to spend that winter in New York and rented a room. It rained like hell, but I was very happy.

One day, I was talking to someone in the Lincoln veteran's association office when a call came in from the furrier's union. They wanted help on the picket line and were offering the job to any unemployed vet. He turned to me and asked how long I would be in New York. I told him I figured on staying until spring, and he gave me a note to take to the union hall.

I was paired up with a Jewish boy to picket the smaller sweat shops in the garment and furriers district. We spelled each other off and were paid two dollars a day, a lot of money for that time. I would often go to the morning movies on my time off. Movies were on twenty-four hours a day and cost only ten cents in the mornings.

The businesses we picketed were family affairs, and safety was not a factor. My girlfriend told me of the unsafe conditions where she worked in a sweatshop making dresses for piecework wages.[128] [129] Anybody who parted their hair the wrong way was fired. It was not long before things improved, because many of the garment factories got contracts to make military uniforms, even while the US was officially neutral.

One time, I was with a friend and we saw a worker rolling a rack of fur coats along the street to take for finishing. The pay was low, because business owners often hired illegal immigrants so they could use them any way they wanted. We stopped him and asked if he was interested in joining the union. He turned to a big Irish cop and said, "Do I have to answer these questions?"

The cop said, "No! Tell them to go to hell."

Another time, the union recommended that I be hired as a furrier's representative. The job was to arrange skins for sale in lots to be bid on. I had a pretty interesting life that winter. I learnt a lot and made good friends.

It was also New York, in a Greenwich Village art gallery, where I met the artist who, thirty-seven years later, became the key to unlocking my memories—the one whose enigmatic portrait had so intrigued me.

At our very first meeting, the artist had wondered why I used "dislike," not "hate," when he asked how I would feel about living near the noise of the elevated train. Through our many talks about my past, he would come to know that I reserved "hate" for the fascists who slaughtered hundreds of thousands of innocent men, women, and children in Spain to ensure the rule of a handful of capitalists and landed nobility.[130]

Knowing as much as he did about me, I wonder if the artist ever painted my portrait. If he did, it is lost to time. I can thank him, though, for unleashing my buried memories, not only those decades ago in New York but again in 1977 in Peterborough, as I write these words.

In March 1941, I left New York and took the bus to Toronto. I could have hitched a ride to a border crossing with no customs agents, but I took my chances.

At the border, I was asked for proof I was Canadian. I had no proof, so they took me off the bus, searched my luggage, and sent me to see the head of customs.

I was truthful and told him I had entered the States without going through customs and that I had been working in New York as a picket. He asked, "What have you been doing these past few years?"

I told him I had been to Spain. He must have been a sympathizer, because he expressed interest, and we had a long chat.[131] To ensure I was Canadian, he asked me for the names of the provinces and their premiers. I answered to his satisfaction and was let go.

I easily found work in Toronto as a sign painter, and then headed to Peterborough where jobs were plentiful because of war contracts. The Great Depression was finally over.[132]

Jim Higgins was employed on outside sign painting at E. L. Ruddy, the company that dominated Toronto's downtown billboards, from March 26, 1941 until January 10, 1942.[133]

Chapter 17
A WOMAN LIKE NO OTHER

THINGS WERE LOOKING UP. Not only did I have a job, but I was heading into the happiest time of my life: I met Reta Palliser who was to become my wife.[134]

It was at a dance at the Brock Street Arena in Peterborough. I usually went stag to public dances and had no trouble getting someone to dance with me. This time was no different, but I quickly realized that Reta herself was quite different from any woman I had known: she was a Liberal, came from an entrepreneurial family, and had a BA from Queens University. Despite these differences, we really enjoyed each other's company, and I was surprised I could talk freely with her. During the next few months, I told Reta about my politics and experiences in the Depression; things she knew little about.

We were attracted to each other and enjoyed many things in common, including the arts, live theatre, and the same kind of music. Each of us had travelled across Canada more than once, though in very different ways. In the 1920s, her family had taken several two-month summer camping trips across the prairies and mountains. I saw those sights from trains; sometimes while riding the rails.

When I met Reta, she was working in the payroll department at Westclox and living with a nurse. It was from her that Reta received the first sour note about me: a warning that I was not good enough for her. The nurse would not be the only one.

On a nice Sunday weather-wise, Reta would bring a lunch and we would set out for Lakefield along the River Road, stopping for a picnic at one of the locks on the Otonabee River. We discussed everything under the sun during those long walks. It was surprising how many things we agreed upon. If we differed, we respected the other's point of view.

Reta Palliser and Jim Higgins during their courtship, probably on the Otonabee River somewhere between Peterborough and Lakefield.

One Sunday, we talked about the Bible, and Reta asked how I knew so much about it. I told her that it was the first book I had really read deeply, and that I interpreted it in my own way. I also said I found my faith, not in organized religion, but in nature. Though I was not a church goer, this was important to Reta, a United Church member, if she were to accept me as her partner.

Reta understood me better than anyone and even mothered me at times with my problems. I am sure that, if I had a mate other than her, I would not have had a family. Most people do not know that I am emotional, because I hide it well, but I trusted her and could relax in her company.

She saw it upset me to see a dog that had been killed by a car and a few months after I bought my own car, I swerved to miss a cat, lost control, and the car landed on its side in the ditch. It was a reaction that could have killed us both. She must have thought these things strange for one who had seen so many people slaughtered.

Later that fall, we decided to get married. By then, we knew we could compromise over any problems and agreed our union would be a partnership. By the time she asked me to meet her parents, I had saved enough for the car. It was an old DeSoto, built like a tank.

We made it to Campbellford that Saturday without a breakdown. When I met her parents, I knew immediately they accepted me. That feeling was reinforced through the years when we visited and her mother would prepare dishes she knew I liked.

Reta's mother and I had a special relationship—I called her "mother" and she told me something once that even her own family did not know and that secret will die with me. Despite her parents' acceptance, not everyone in Reta's family thought I was good enough for her.

I promised to do everything I could to make our partnership happy and successful. Before our marriage, we agreed that she would give up her job at Westclox and devote herself to making a home for us. She was reluctant to quit her job, but we agreed that if conditions became too tough, she would work part-time.

Our wedding was a lovely affair in her parents' home. We took our vows under a flower-covered arch on Saturday, November 7, 1942. Among the guests were Phil and May Dawes, strangers who had taken me in when I came back from the Spanish Civil War. Now Phil was my best man.

After the reception, Reta's mother drove us to Havelock to catch the train to Toronto. After swerving to miss a cow, she was too upset to drive further, so I drove the rest of the way. We made it to Toronto without further incident, but when we were ushered to our room at the King Edward Hotel, we had to laugh—instead of the double bed we were expecting, there were two singles.

That evening, we went to a play at the Royal Alexandra Theatre, courtesy of the Dawes. The play did not hold our attention (maybe something other than the play was on our minds), and we left at intermission. The next morning, we chuckled as we rumpled the unused bed. That was our honeymoon. I was back to work Monday morning.

Our first home together was two rooms, and we shared a bathroom with the family we rented from. There was no kitchen, and the only water was in the bathroom. Cooking was done on a two-burner, table-top stove. I bought a small icebox, and the iceman delivered twenty pounds of ice twice a week. It was tough, but we only came closer together in our love for each other.

Reta became pregnant that following spring, and my next task was to convince the higher ups where I worked at CGE—Canadian General Electric—that with a baby on the way, I needed a wartime house.[135]

Janette was delivered January 17, 1944. The doctor had suggested I wait at home. Reading was no good, so I tried painting. I had been dabbling with paints for a few years by then. The painting was a watercolour of an imagined rocky landscape. Needless to say, I made a complete mess of it.

I was successful in my bid for a wartime house, and we moved in the week after Janette's birth. It had a stove and fridge! Although we did not have much furniture, we bought what we needed at Cherney's, a second-hand store on Hunter Street. The old man pushed his handcart around to pick up "junk" for his sons to sell.

Jim and Reta holding their first-born daughter, Janette.

Later that year, I was laid off at CGE where I had been working in the tool room for twelve hours a day. (I was also trying to organize the workers.) The next day, I landed a higher-paying job in the machine shop at the Outboard Marine Company, a manufacturer of outboard motors for boats. They were having trouble filling a specialized job, and I went on to prove myself, meeting their expectations.

Reta and I came to an understanding, and I reduced my union activity to once a week. I was still working plenty of overtime and saving for a place of our own. In buying our first property, in a way, I was realizing my long-ago dream of homesteading on the prairies, only this was a twenty-acre hobby farm on the edge of Peterborough. It had a barn, an apple orchard, and an old bare-bones farmhouse. We had a cow named Daisy, a horse named Charlie, and a rooster with a flock of chickens.

Life was good on our "country estate" and Reta was very happy there. Her family visited often, and we made friends with our neighbours. During the day, the women visited one another, and sometimes in the evening, one or another of the families would visit or invite us over to their home. There was always lots of joking and laughter.

Although it was a new and strange way of life for Reta, for me it was just another challenge to overcome—only this time I had somebody to encourage me and always be by my side. I softened, and our feelings for each other became even stronger.

Sometimes Reta expressed concern that I was overdoing it. Besides working a lot of overtime, I worked late in the evenings in the garden or in the field I plowed and cropped with the help of faithful old Charlie.

To keep our heads above water, I sold eggs and chickens, mostly to my mates, and on weekends I delivered to their homes. I also sold apples and other produce to Routley's, a grocery store in town. I made the windfall apples into cider, using a hand-operated mill, and on Saturdays in the fall, customers arrived with their own containers to catch the juice as it flowed from the mill.

Our son, Jim, was born twenty-two months after Janette. We decided that two children were all we could afford, so we consulted our doctor about birth control and followed his advice.

Jim on his "country estate" feeding Charlie, the horse, while holding his son, "Jamie."

Then—so much for 1940s birth control—we had twins. Barbara and Margaret arrived February 3, 1948. The storms that followed that March were wicked. The snow plow was half-buried on another road, and the drifts were often within three feet of the tops of the phone and hydro poles. I bought snowshoes so I could get to the edge of town where a buddy would pick me up and take me to work.

Our "country estate" was now too small, and we became concerned about our children's education. It was time to move back into Peterborough. Besides—something I did not mention—our water came from a well and our "bathroom" was an outhouse. We now had four children under five years of age and needed the facilities a city home could provide.

I was looking for a house in good repair but location was the most important thing to Reta. We were finally shown 216 McDonnel Street, a nine-room house built in the early 1800s. The situation was ideal—close to schools, library, a park, city hall, and downtown—but the house was in bad shape. The front verandah was falling down, and the soft places on the pine floors had worn away, leaving knots sticking up. It had a coal furnace of sorts, and the electric wiring was about the first installed in Peterborough. I knew I had a job to do.

We moved in December 15, 1948, a Wednesday, and I took the day off work. I more than made up for it by working that Saturday at time and a half, and Sunday at two and a half times pay. For the next two years, I worked day and night, which is probably why I developed a stomach ulcer. I was put on a special diet, quit smoking, and even gave up the occasional beer I enjoyed before supper on a hot day.

The ulcer meant I could not take medication for a nervous condition I had.[136] I became irritable at work, and my foreman found it best to leave me alone. I also had a row with the factory's works manager, because I refused to be timed on a tough job. I really blew my top. An hour later, while everyone watched, instead of firing me, he apologised. He shook my hand and said top management had asked him to make peace with me. When he left me, he said, "No hard feelings, Jim," and I agreed. That is how I got the nickname, "the old warhorse."

That evening, after supper, I worked in the garden. I was always relaxed there, and it was where Reta and I talked over our problems away from the children. She came out, and after telling her what had happened, she was firm that I see my doctor the next morning. He told me to go home and work in the garden and called the company to say that I would not be at work for at least ten days.

By this time, I had made a bedroom for our son, Jim, by cutting the large bathroom in two. This was a major job where I needed a plumber and an electrician. The hot water tank was moved to the cellar, and the location of the bathtub, toilet, and washbasin had to be changed. Then I cut through the exterior wall and installed a window for the new bedroom.

Thinking back, I wonder how I did so much in such a short time. Without Reta, I could not have done it as she looked after the children, did all the cooking and cleaning, and anything else that would interfere with my projects.

Then it all came to a sudden stop. The overwork Reta had tried to keep me from landed me in the hospital. It was early January 1951. I had gone to the bathroom in the middle of the night and got halfway to the toilet when I went down. I fell forward, and the top of my right eye hit the toilet bowl, causing a deep gash. Reta found me, cleaned me up, and insisted I see a doctor the next morning.

Stubborn as I am, I went to work. As soon as the plant nurse saw the wound, she sent me to a doctor to get it stitched, and he immediately got me in to see Dr. Leslie Calvert who was treating me for my ulcer. Dr. Calvert said that I had lost so much blood through internal bleeding that he could not understand how I could still be on my feet. "Hell, Jim, did you not feel tired and weak during the last few days?"

He phoned the Civic Hospital and told them he was bringing in an emergency case. Blood was dripping into me for the next few days, and on the tenth day, I was on the table for four hours while the medical team took out two-thirds of my stomach.

For the next few days, I had three nurses on shift around the clock. Their pay was not covered by insurance, so I paid them myself. I was surprised that it was only a dollar an hour, since I knew the sweeper in the factory was earning more than that. With their training and credentials, I thought nurses should be making much more. I decided to write a letter to the editor of the Peterborough Examiner.

I was accustomed to writing letters to newspaper editors wherever I lived. By the time I met Reta, I had worked out a system. The first draft would be a dozen pages, and I would rewrite it two or three times to make it, at most, two pages. In the first draft of this letter, as usual, I went into a lot of detail. Reta read it and asked what I was trying to say. Within a minute I told her. She said, "Why not just write it that way?" I did as she suggested and received more phone calls about that letter to the editor than I did for any other.

Our youngest child, Susan, was born April 25, 1955. Everyone loved her. It was a new experience for her brother and sisters to have a baby in the home, since they had been born so close together.

Then, a devastating blow: Reta was diagnosed with breast cancer. On July 29, 1961, she was gone. She was fifty-one. It tore me up inside. Janette did not understand why I did not keep her portrait up in the living room. I could not. It was just too painful. I did not want to break down in front of my children.

Before she left us, Reta asked me to promise to keep the family together and not let anyone take Susan away. She was also realistic and suggested I marry again. Today, as I write this at age seventy, I am glad I did not. The family did indeed stay together until one-by-one our children left home. I tried my best, but I know that at times I was rough to live with.

On Christmas Day 1973, Jim surprised his family by taking them to the Roy Studio for a family portrait. He had convinced Mr. Roy to open because it was the only time he would have everyone together. No family portrait was taken while Reta was alive. Rear: (Son) Jim, Susan, Barbara. Front: Janette, Jim, Maggie.

To adapt the words of a popular song, "We did it our way." Our marriage worked because it was a partnership. We did not have any fairy-tale notions and were realistic about the ups and downs. Together, we launched five wonderful, understanding children into this rough and tough world who have made my life happier. I like to think we did a real good job together. I have not mentioned much about the fun part of our partnership, but it was always there. We joked and laughed and had good times.

Loving Reta was a pleasure. There is not a day that passes when I do not think back on those happy times.

Jim's beloved wife and partner, Reta Florence Higgins, nee Palliser (1910-1961)
Etched onto their joint tombstone are the words,
"MUTUAL LOVE: THE CROWN OF ALL OUR BLISS."

Epilogue
SECRETS—BUT NO LIES

AROUND 1960, WHERE HIS memoir leaves off, my father slipped on a spot of oil at work and went down on his back, breaking it. Over the next few years, he had two major surgeries. It was just before his first surgery that our mother died of cancer at age fifty-one, leaving him with five children still at home. Four of us were teenagers and could fend for ourselves when Dad was in rehab in Toronto for months at a time, but Susan was only six. In retrospect, it was toughest on her.

Dad lived another twenty plus years with chronic pain, unable to work at his regular job. He still needed money to support us and for a while his employer, Outboard Marine Corporation (OMC), accommodated his disability, giving him a job as night watchman in a warehouse, where he could lie down between rounds. In 1969, at age sixty-two, the company forced him to retire.

Dad hasn't written about his union and political activities after he moved to Peterborough, but he was very involved, both with the United Electrical Workers at Canadian General Electric and the United Steelworkers at Outboard Marine. He once told a journalist that his opponents at work would whisper against him because of Spain—that he had just as much trouble with the union executive as with management—but that didn't stop him.[137]

He became chief steward and advocated for workers' compensation claims. He also held positions with the Peterborough Labour Council, including Secretary and Chair of the Education Committee. He refused at least one work promotion so he could stay true to his union mates, and after retiring and seeing Outboard Marine pensioner rights being eroded, he fought a public battle for those as well.

On the political front, I saw him excited to be working hard on Walter Pitman's successful 1960 by-election campaign for the New Party, the interim name for the New Democratic Party (NDP), and he became a lifetime member.

I always thought his stomach ulcer was due to his union battles and the stress of overwork. I wonder now if the ulcers weren't a manifestation of battles of another kind (post-traumatic stress from his war years), though he once told a journalist he never talked about the war, and never even dreamed about it. "I'm glad I went over there. I'm proud of what I did, but I put the war behind me."[138] It may be that surety that saved him from any nightmares.

Before he became disabled, it was apparent Dad loved his garden, and I loved "helping" him. I have memories of trays of seedlings crowding the second-floor sunporch in the spring; everything from petunias and marigolds to tomatoes and cucumbers.

My favourite memories, though, were of Sundays after services with our mother at George Street United Church, when we went into the countryside for picnics, berry picking, or spring walks in the woods to enjoy, but never pick, wild-flowers. Now, I realize, he was introducing us to his "church."

And it's also only now that I realize the sacrifice he made when I decided to return to school at age eighteen after working for a year. This meant I stopped paying room and board just as he was disabled, struggling financially, and coping with the loss of our mother.

Not once did he say anything to dissuade me as I completed grade thirteen and went on to what was then a one-year program at Peterborough Teacher's College. By January of that second year, he knew I'd run through my savings. When I came down for breakfast the morning of my birthday, under my plate was a hundred-dollar bill.

In Dad's later years, his joys were listening to the CBC, reading a wide range of library books, and spending summers at the "cottage" near McCracken's Landing on Stoney Lake, a cabin he rented from Bill and Marguerite Hamilton. There, amongst a community of friends who looked out for him, including the Hamiltons and George and Sheila Hall, he enjoyed peaceful times fishing in his small boat and training chipmunks to eat out of his hand.

138

And so it was, at Christmas 1976, that we children pressed him to write his story for us. He wrote throughout 1977, and in September, passed on his stories about the Spanish Civil War to the Mac-Pap Veterans' association, leading to Manuel Alvarez finding his "tall soldier," as described in the prologue. They reunited in the spring of 1978 with international news coverage.

Jim Higgins and Manuel Alvarez reunited in Peterborough Ontario on May 19, 1978. They are flanked by Janette (left) and Susan (right). Daughter, Barbara, took the picture.

Manuel went home to Vancouver to write *The Tall Soldier,* which was published to critical acclaim in 1980. This time there was even more news coverage and the two were interviewed by the likes of CBC greats Peter Gzowski and Barbara Frum. As Dad said, "We both thought the story was bigger than ourselves … that in a way, Manuel represented a grateful Spanish people, and that if I am the hero they say I am, then every single person who volunteered to fight for democracy in Spain was a hero."

As a side note, Dad lost his sisters' addresses during the 1930s; perhaps they were in the packsack he relinquished during the war. Their names were Emily Jane Higgens (or Higgins) and Kate Louisa Higgens, who "somehow became Freda in her letters to me."

Kate, who was six years older, married a Canadian First World War veteran whose last name was Springer, and he remembered them living in Vancouver. He could not remember Emily Jane's husband's name. She was three years older than Dad, and on one occasion, he referred to her as Doris.

By the early 1980s, Dad was frail, in severe chronic pain, and suffering from the effects of TIAs—small strokes—no doubt, at least in part, because he was a lifelong smoker. The man born as Harry James Thomas Higgens died September 18, 1982 at age seventy-five. The name on his death certificate was James Henry Higgins. Though his name may have varied throughout his life, his ideals and convictions did not.

When we were planning his small graveside funeral at Peterborough's Little Lake Cemetery, my sister Susan found a hand-written poem amongst his papers, which she read as part of the ceremony. It took me a while to realize he had paraphrased the Ralph Waldo Emerson poem, "What is Success?" A more fitting epitaph he could not have had.

Success in Life

To appreciate beauty.

To find the best in others—a tough one.

To have accomplished a task: bringing up a family, planting a garden, or trying to improve a social condition.

To earn the honest respect of your critics and to understand false friends—another tough one.

To have the respect of persons who have some intelligence.

To have the affection of my children.

To love sincerely and find time to laugh.

To know that even one person has breathed easier because I have lived.

Jim Higgins

HAVING BEEN IMMERSED IN my father's memoir, I'd come to understand the things I mentioned in the prologue—where his prowess in the water came from, why he biked across the United States, and I'd gained insight into why he would paint the image of a dead woman with blood pooling on the ground.

According to his RCMP file, Jim Higgins was "extremely well built."[139] His physique, evident in this photo, would explain his ability to carry heavy machine guns for long periods. As for his swimming prowess, Jim's children rarely saw him swim, but in his later years, he once startled Susan by diving into a lake. To her astonishment, he quietly surfaced and glided through the water using a confident crawl, as though free from infirmity.

I also had a much deeper understanding of how his ideals were forged and how strongly held they were. It seemed I had most of the answers. But then a niggling thought—perhaps there was something I still didn't know. Curiously, he had commented on audiotape that he would be carrying two secrets to his grave.

I was pretty sure I knew the first was one told to him by our grandmother, but what about the second? Was it relevant to his memoir? Could it have to do with why he was chosen to be Major Cecil-Smith's commissar on the ship home? Though I'd uncovered Dad's role in intelligence, suggesting he had a closer connection to Edward Cecil-Smith than did the usual soldier, that part still puzzled me.

Then, a bombshell. Included amongst Comintern—Communist International—documents for the International Brigades in Russian archives, was Dad's exit questionnaire. In the space for "political and trade union organisations of which you are a member," he'd written, "Communist Party of Canada. Pleasant Hill Branch. Saskatoon."[140]

What!? I went back, looked closely, and saw that he never outright denied being a member of the Communist Party. It took a while to digest, but here's how I view it, knowing my father's character, noting his precision in choosing his words, and accounting for the tenor of the times.

I believe the kernel of Jim Higgins's truth is best captured in what he wrote about his decision to go to Spain in Chapter Five, "While I could not fully commit myself to any political party or organization, I did associate with many causes that I thought were worthy, such as workers' rights and trying to improve the lot of the single unemployed. This seemed like a worthy cause, if ever there was one. I knew the Communist Party was involved, and had even been asked many times to become an official member, but resisted because I did not want to be tied down, to become a robot. I wanted to be independent and decide myself if a cause was worth fighting for."

In the 1930s, the Communist Party of Canada (CPC) was one of many organizations on the left, and there were countless threads and connections amongst them. In 1935, in line with the Comintern's "dramatic change of political direction," the CPC built a Popular Front Against Fascism, hence broadening its appeal.[141] The Popular Front strategy also helps explain the broad public support for those who fought in Spain.

Fascism was a threat to western democracies long before the Second World War, but their leaders did not see it that way. They admired Hitler and Mussolini's accomplishments; it was the "Red Menace" that concerned them. Citizens like Jim Higgins, and others in Canada and around the world, had a tough choice. If they wanted to fight fascism, they had to defy their own governments' hastily enacted foreign enlistment laws designed to keep them out of Spain. The fact is, it was only because of the Comintern's impressive organizational efforts to support volunteers in getting to Spain that the renowned International Brigades came into being.

In light of this, I realize my father's words were always carefully chosen. My guess is that he thought the best way for him to support the people of Spain was to become "tied down," but only for a short while, and join the communist party. It seems that, in his own independent mind, he could claim he was not an "official" member since he was not "card-carrying."

Here's another example of words carefully chosen. In the chapter about crossing the Pyrenees, he said of the three documents he turned over when he enlisted in Paris, "None were from the communist party." How could that be true in light of this new revelation? I knew him to be honest to a fault.

Well, it turns out, it probably is "true." He was just being evasive, a tactic he admitted to using when we children asked him questions about his past. A Communist Party of Spain report has revealed that Jim Higgins is "characterized by the following good qualities: Secretary of the Unemployed Movement in Saskatoon, Sask."[142]

Aha! The Unemployed Movement of Saskatoon was one of the front organizations for the CPC and—along with letters from the Co-operative Commonwealth Federation (CCF) and the Saskatoon Labour Council—a letter from the Unemployed Movement would have been what he gave Comintern organizers in Paris.

An underlying theme that marks my father's feelings about the CPC from early on, seems to be his less-than-favourable opinion of the leadership, despite sharing certain ideals with the party, especially when they took their new direction in 1935. In 1930, he described them as "armchair generals" and later opined that some made "lousy officers" in the Spanish Civil War.

Then, shortly after the Mac-Paps' return in 1939, there were problems with the CPC leadership over plans to publish a book. Dad hasn't written about this in his memoir. I only know because of a note buried amongst his papers. Several veterans had been asked to write about their experiences in Spain, and the pieces he wrote in 1939 are now part of this book. I knew the plans to publish that year had fallen by the wayside. I didn't know why, maybe something to do with everyone being preoccupied with the Second World War. At least that was what I'd read in other books.[143] [144]

Dad's note gave the real reason. Here is an excerpt, "Although I wrote some of my memoir in 1939, the material was not published. The planned book was halted because the writers, who were gathering material from the vets, disagreed with the political editors ... the writers wanted to have the pros as well as the cons, incorporated into the book, but the politicals wanted only the good points written."[145] [146]

In Dad's parlance, the "politicals" were CPC officials, because for the most part, the "writers," including him at that point in April 1939, were also members of the communist party. By May, he had quit. I know this because it's in my father's Royal Canadian Mounted Police (RCMP) file, which I finally received in 2019.

The file was opened in 1935 when he led the delegation to the Rigg Commission. It confirmed that he joined the Communist Party of Canada in 1937, a few months before he left for Spain. Another report indicates he quit the party in May 1939, so shortly after his return.[147] [148] This is in line with the experience of many volunteers. The complexities of that time are often overlooked, but I hope my father's story gives nuance and dimension to all who put their lives on the line in Spain for their ideals.

Research by Michael Petrou shows that "approximately 76 percent of Canadians in Spain were communists—either full-fledged party members or members of the Young Communist League. More than 90 per cent of those... became communists during the 1930s, and enrolment was highest in 1935 and 1936—years of heightened militancy on the part of unemployed Canadians and of the Communist Party's strategy of a popular front. It is unclear if some future volunteers joined the party specifically as a result of the Spanish Civil War, but given the spike in enlistment in 1936, it is reasonable to assume this might have been the case."[149]

It would be reasonable to assume this was the case for Jim Higgins; his political affiliation was first with the CCF (and its early 1930s predecessor organizations), and then with the NDP. In his lifetime, that labelled him a social democrat.

Above all, it seems clear to me that, crucial to his way of thinking, social equality in a democracy requires one to actively challenge capitalism and that can involve making difficult decisions and putting your life on the line.

I worried for a bit that I might be disloyal in "outing" him on what I believe to be his second secret. But if I hadn't, the first scholar to delve into his memoir would have. I decided to be the first so I could address his reasoning.

My conclusion is that, for Jim Higgins, the end justified the means. In 1937, he made a pragmatic decision to join the Communist Party of Canada for some limited period of time so he could contribute fully to a cause he was passionate about.

Perhaps the most fitting label for Jim Higgins is the one he used in his military book—anti-fascist—but I will give him the last word. It comes from his first media interview, given in 1975 when Franco died. When asked if he was a communist, he replied, "I'm an individualist, have been all my life."[150]

He certainly saw himself that way in 1939 when he wrote about being uncharacteristically open with "Bill" in the climb over the Pyrenees, "Over the two days that Bill and I talked, I discovered we had a lot in common, especially that we were both individualists. Neither of us was a card-carrying political member, but both of us were connected with movements on the left. We were trusted in the inner circles of certain parties and invited to their meetings."

The heavy RCMP surveillance wound down by the late 1950s (his file even includes the full names and birthdates of his five children), but the last document in his file was a feature article in *The Montreal Gazette* about him and Manuel Alvarez. It was dated 1980—meaning he was in their sights for forty-five years.

I think it can be understood why Jim Higgins was evasive and why he felt forced to submit to societal pressures in view of the spiteful and unjust allegations against "communists" unleashed by McCarthyism in the United States during the Cold War and which spread to places like Canada. He was protecting his family.

I withheld his communist party affiliation until now because I didn't want to "out" him in a buried footnote. I wanted the opportunity to write this longest footnote of all. I can only hope I got it right.

ONCE THE COLD WAR began to wind down in the late 1970s, and the RCMP decided old Spanish Civil War vets didn't pose much of a threat, the surviving Mac-Paps and their supporters advocated for pensions at the federal level.

Jim Higgins and Manuel Alvarez were in the thick of it when the veterans' delegation went to Ottawa. If not pensions, they sought at least some kind of official recognition that they weren't criminals for flouting the Foreign Enlistment Act to fight fascism, especially since the Canadian government was forced to fight the very same enemy in the Second World War.

Manuel gave copies of his book to the assembled Mac-Paps in Ottawa, saying, "Republican Spain and I are (proud) of you and your sacrifice. Unfortunately Canada is not. I hope the Canadian government and people will ... honour all the Mac-Paps for what they did ... I will be joyful and finally know release."[151] Another news report of their quest ended with, "'We were all tall soldiers,' Higgins says, shifting his cane from one hand to the other and waiting for Canada to answer."[152]

The pensions didn't happen, and Manuel was to know no joy. He died of a heart attack before official recognition of any kind was afforded the Mac-Paps. I am truly grateful that my father lived long enough to be found and thanked by Manuel.

Spurred by citizen efforts in the early 1990s, provincial NDP governments in Ontario and British Columbia lent their support to Mac-Pap memorials in Toronto and Victoria.

Around the same time, Sudbury architect Jules Paivio, one of the last surviving Mac-Pap veterans, spearheaded the drive for a national memorial in Ottawa. Private monies were raised—my family contributed—and the Governor General of Canada, the Right Honourable Adrienne Clarkson, became involved.

Designed by another Sudbury architect, Oryst Sawchuk, the memorial features a sixteen-foot-high rusted metal profile of a Promethean figure with his fist raised to the Spanish sun. The figure is mounted on a low stone wall inscribed with the names of most of the Canadian volunteers including "Jimmy Higgins."

The clenched fist salute was used by Spanish Republicans in opposition to the flat palmed Nazi salute of Franco's rebels. Today, it continues as a symbol of resistance.

Madame Clarkson was responsible for securing the spot on Green Island, just west of the Prime Minister's residence, where you will find the memorial. It was

The Ottawa Memorial for Canadians who fought with the Mackenzie-Papineau Battalion was dedicated by the Right Honourable Adrienne Clarkson in 2001. The small square stone in front was placed by Spain's Ambassador to Canada in 2011. With Franco dead in 1975 and democracy restored, the Spanish government offered all who fought with the International Brigades honorary Spanish citizenship. They are celebrated in Spain to this day. Photo Credit: Shawn Micallef

dedicated by her on October 20, 2001, a beautiful, sunny day. I was there with my sister, Susan, along with a few hundred others.

My father was long dead by then, as were most Mac-Paps, but for me, Madame Clarkson's speech gave them as much official validation, even vindication, as they have ever received, or perhaps ever will. She ended with, "Today we are giving members of the Mackenzie-Papineau Battalion a lasting memorial—here where it should be, in their own land."

I was surprised to find myself overcome by emotion. As I wept, I felt a strange release that my father was at peace. Finally, it was recognized, in a symbolically significant way, that he and his comrades had done the right thing.

Janette Higgins

ABOUT THE EDITING

THERE WILL BE THOSE who question how I went about editing a draft manuscript written by someone long dead. Did I put words in his mouth? Did I change his voice? How did I deal with the inevitable puzzles, mysteries, questions, and mistakes?

Long before retirement, I typed the material my father had written into a computer, waiting for when I'd have time to tackle what I knew was mine to do. William French's words, "Heroes deserve histories, too," never left me.

In early 2017, I listened to ten audio-taped radio interviews with Manuel and my father. By July, I was working full time on the project. The first step was to organize the mass of material—archival documents, piles of newspaper clippings, hand-written stories and typed versions from 1939 and 1977, in no particular order, and thirty more audio tapes of my father reading the chapters he had written, again in no particular order.

In my first stabs at editing, I was able to clarify a few things, but it was still a confusing story and there were hints of problems to come—this piece didn't seem to have an ending, and something about that story didn't make sense. This was going to need more work than I'd thought.

My next task was to listen to the audio tapes my father made in 1980 reading what he'd written. By then, he had limited capacity to write and revise. Maybe I'd get some answers to the questions that were surfacing. Beyond that, I badly needed his permission to do what I knew needed to be done. I had started out with the sense that I shouldn't change a word. I knew I had to get over that hurdle.

Luckily, I got much of what I needed. My father ad-libbed clarifications, *most* of the missing chapter endings, and I learned how some of his material went missing. Sadly, it's unlikely it will ever be recovered.

Most importantly, I received the permission I craved. Several times, when recording, he commented on the need for the material to be edited, the most pertinent being, "It needs to be rewritten and edited. If I can't rewrite it, it needs to be edited by someone else."

Did I put words in his mouth? It took a while to decide, but yes, there were times when I chose to do so. An example can be found in the first chapter. The opening line is his, augmented by his ad lib about there being no midwife at his birth over the pub. The next two factual sentences are mine. Another example can be found in Chapter 16 when "he" refers back to the artist—it was my way of bringing the memoir full circle using his comments on "hate" from another piece he'd written.

I also inserted information from his ad libs, media interviews, 1930s newspaper accounts, and facts from his RCMP file. For example, I hadn't known he was in Regina when the stock market crashed. It came from one of his newspaper interviews. And in June 2019, at Library and Archives Canada, in the Mackenzie-Papineau Collection, I found several missing paragraphs for Chapter 11, describing his experience at the end of the Retreats.

Did I change his voice? I hope not. An example; he did not use contractions in his manuscript, and at one point early on, I started contracting words so it would sound less formal. After thinking about it, I changed them back, except where he was quoting conversations. He used British spellings, such as *learnt,* and I kept those as well.

In the main, I was cutting redundancy and moving things around for better flow as well as researching and correcting any mistakes I could identify. That was the easy part.

When it came to the chronology, it was like solving a complicated jigsaw puzzle. Every week seemed to bring some new revelation, and even two and a half years after I started, I was discovering critical pieces and figuring out where they fit.

The documenting of his story has shown me that, whilst he may have written variations and made honest mistakes—for example, on timing—I never found that he embellished; in fact, quite the contrary. He was modest to a fault. This aligns with my memory of an honest and humble man with strong opinions about what was right. In fact, his modesty often got in the way of clarity, and the documentation has helped me shape his writing to remove confusion for the reader.

Despite my familial relationship, I tried to maintain a sceptical eye. For example, I could find no documentation of his leadership role in the Saskatoon by-election and I wondered about it. The "aha!" moment came from his RCMP file, which verified he was on the executive committee of the United Reform Movement. Unfortunately, I've been unable to locate W. G. Brown's diary to check for more corroborating evidence.

The truly hazy part of his story, short on details and with little, even conflicting, evidence, is what he was doing after Prime Minister Negrin withdrew the International Brigades in September 1938. He says he and José Díaz Artacho stayed on to fight in the Spanish Army and explained that the 5th Army Corps destroyed documentation for people like him. It's also conceivable that there was some kind of cover up. I know in my heart that he did stay on, not only because of what I know about his integrity, but because so much else has panned out. I accept that some Spanish Civil War scholars will be skeptical.

As for my father's memory, with so much information available about the way memory works, I've come to believe that his was more accurate and detailed than many. Certainly, judging by the supporting documentation, he had a far better memory than I do. Of course, that doesn't mean it was perfect.

He was also good at knowing what to leave in and what to leave out, judging by the stories that show signs he rewrote them several times. In my view, had he written and revised his manuscript when healthy, with the help of an editor who asked probing questions and encouraged reflection, it would have been in first-rate shape.

In the end, I can't be sure that every piece of the puzzle is in its rightful place and a few critical pieces are still missing. I'm sure I've made mistakes, and in reworking some of his words, may have misconstrued my father's intent or meaning. I humbly acknowledge that perfection is not possible and take full responsibility for the mistakes that remain.

Janette Higgins

ACKNOWLEDGMENTS

I KNEW MY FATHER'S story was an important reflection of 1930s Canadian history, but it took a host of archivists, historians, and others, to make it what it is.

First to read an early version were sister, Susan Higgins, and friend, Jan de Crespigny. I am grateful for the considerable care they took to provide detailed feedback. After a few more go-throughs, it went out to writers, academics and journalists —Jason Webster, Michael Petrou, Jim Turk, Tom Alderman, and Tori Owen. All were encouraging, and each had a comment or thought which improved the manuscript or enlightened my understanding; though the benefit of hindsight shows it was a bit early to send it to such an august group. Heartfelt thanks to all. Jim Turk went the extra mile and his influential support for my father's story is much appreciated.

Then came Facebook. I joined in August 2018 and within weeks people who are key to the accuracy of this book — as much as that is possible — came forward. Chris Brooks with the Abraham Lincoln Brigade Archives in New York, and Ray Hoff a driving force behind remembering Canadian volunteers in the Spanish Civil War, provided documentation that solved mysteries, established most of the timeline, and took the manuscript to new levels. Thank you, Chris and Ray. You've done yeoman's work.

Tyler Wentzell, Toronto author and military historian, provided thoughtful feedback on the manuscript. He was always there to answer my questions and happy to explore the connections between my father and Mac-Pap commander, Edward Cecil-Smith, the subject of his new biography, *Not for King or Country*. Our two-hour "coffee-break" discussions always left me invigorated. Tyler, you have a special place in my heart.

Valencian, Mariado Hinojosa Poipín, responded enthusiastically when I asked her to have a look in Valencian archives to see if she could find anything about José Díaz Artacho and Captain José Medina Lopez, the two Spaniards who meant so much to my father. I was elated when she came up with documentation. Jorge Marco, at the University of Bath, read the manuscript, confirmed that Jim Higgins was with intelligence, and was quick to respond to my queries. To Mariado and Jorge, *mi sincero agradecimiento*.

Murray Hogben was a journalist with the Kingston Whig Standard when the publicity broke about my father's rescue of Manuel Alvarez. Most news reports simply retold their incredible story. A few journalists wrote feature articles, but it was Hogben's 1981 piece that contained gold. I am indebted to him for asking my father many of the questions I could not.

Thanks are also due to Elizabeth Seitz at the University of Regina Archives who sent scans of my father's documents and writings held there. I already had most of it, but not his *Filiacion* form, nor the photograph taken just before he left Spain. I used both in this book.

Others to recognize are Stuart Walsh in England, James Matthews in Ireland, Peter Verburgh in Belgium, Timo Malmi in Finland, David Yorke and John Wainright/Serge Alternes in Canada, and Joan Antonio Montana, Alan Warren, Nick Lloyd, Anna Marti, Oscar Saladie Borraz, Manel Montero Cueto, all in Spain.

My appreciation also goes to journalists and others who told my father that his story was worth publishing. This includes Manuel Alvarez, who left us too soon, Clifford Maynes of the Peterborough Common Press to whom my father gave his first interview in 1975, and the small cadre of history students at Trent University who befriended him, especially Elaine Farley, who not only typed much of his material, but became a friend. You are special people who gave value to my father's true self, not the tamped down version I knew, and for that I am beyond grateful.

My sincere appreciation also extends to the Right Honourable Adrienne Clarkson who took the time to read the manuscript and send thoughtful and encouraging words.

Also, a shout-out to my brother-in-law, Peter McCubbin, for three decades of help on the technical side, and to the many friends who put up with my ramblings over the years.

154

Finally, a huge hug to my siblings—Jim, Maggie, Barbara and Susan—all of whom supported, encouraged and cheered me on, each in their own way. As for Barbara, she lead the pack on that fateful Christmas Day in 1976 when we prevailed upon my father to write about his past. Without her prodding, I doubt you would have this book in your hand.

Janette Higgins

NOTES

THESE NOTES ARE PROVIDED for two reasons: first, to give the general reader a brief historical overview and some interesting bits that add to the story; and second, though not an academic work, to provide academics and historians with relevant sources and citations.

For further information about Higgins's comrades, most will have brief biographies at www.spanishcivilwar.ca/volunteers. In the case of those who were not Canadian (American and Spanish), citations are given.

Abbreviations

ALBA	Abraham Lincoln Brigade Archives, Tamiment Library, New York University, New York City
LAC	Library and Archives Canada, Ottawa
RCMP	Royal Canadian Mounted Police
RCMP File	Jim Higgins's RCMP file held at LAC and redacted by CSIS (Canadian Security Intelligence Service)
RGASPI	Russian State Archive of Socio-Political History
RGASPI Higgins	RGASPI Fond 545. Opis 6. Delo 552. II (Higgins's personnel file, including his exit questionnaire completed by him on November 20, 1938.)

Shortened references:

CM ORIGINAL

Refers to all that remains of Higgins's Original Carnet Militar (Military Book)—two loose pages recording his time with the Mac-Paps during the March 1938 Retreats.

CM REPLICA:

Refers to Higgins's Replica Carnet Militar #76,787A, completed in one hand and dated December 3, 1938, nine weeks after the International Brigades were withdrawn. Pages are loose and many are missing. The entries are often at odds with archival documents cited in the notes. The CM Replica shows he was with the Mac-Paps for the Battle of Teruel, the Retreats, and the Battle of the Ebro, with nothing recorded/remaining for the times he was with the 15th Brigade, 35th Division, Spanish Army, or at Officer Training Schools.

Chapter 1: Orphaned

1   Jim Higgins told his family that "Higgens" was a misspelling on his birth certificate. However, "Higgins" could have been a clerical error made after he was orphaned.

2   In April 1908, when he was ten months old, Higgins's birth father died. By age two, his mother, Annie Maria (Ison) Higgens, was remarried to Ernest Herbert Howell, a builder's plumber. It would have been his stepfather who was killed in the bombing.

Chapter 2: Boom then Bust

3   "Henry James Higgins" arrived in Canada on the *S.S. Megantic* on August 19, 1928 under the Government Harvesting Scheme.

4   Higgins's "group" would have been one that amalgamated in 1932 into the
    Co-operative Commonwealth Federation (CCF), a federation of farmer, labour, and
    socialist parties in western Canada. Higgins was a CCF member for as long as it
    lasted—into the late 1950s.

Chapter 4: We Want Work With Wages

5   By 1932, there were 70,000 single unemployed men in municipal relief camps
    across Canada, many in deplorable condition. Fearing major disorder, R. B. Bennett's
    Conservative government took over the camps in early 1933 and put them under
    the Department of National Defence. New camps were built in isolated areas,
    inmates could not vote, and it was thought they would not organize. In fact, the men
    did organize, and the camps became a focal point for their anger.

6   A temporary tent camp, set up in Spring 1933 at Dundurn, housed six hundred men,
    most from overflowing relief camps in Regina, Saskatoon, and Moose Jaw. The first
    huts at Dundurn were built in late June 1933. The inmates were working on camp
    infrastructure for 20 cents a day plus board. Carpenters, like Higgins, earned more.
    "University Students Serve with Laborers in Jobless Army," *Regina Leader Post*, June
    29, 1933, 13

7   Higgins remembers the huts he built as housing forty men. By 1934, newer
    dormitories at Dundurn housed a hundred men, but eight were half-size, housing
    fifty. These would have been the huts Higgins worked on in 1933. It's likely that five
    bunk beds were later added to each. "New Quarters to be Built at Dundurn Camp,"
    Regina Leader Post, October 24, 1934, 3

8   On a random list of topics, Higgins wrote, "pile driver, Ladder Lake." There was a
    relief camp at Ladder Lake, so it's likely Higgins went there to do more useful work.

9   "Harry Jim Higgins...was agitator in Dundurn Relief Camp and later Single Workers
    Union, and is so recorded in radical files." RCMP File, Report, March 2, 1939

10 In mid-1935, Bennett's conservatives were ousted and the newly elected Liberal
    Prime Minister, Mackenzie King, transferred responsibility for the relief camps from
    the Department of National Defence to the Department of Labour. The new Labour
    Minister established a three-man committee, headed by R. A. Rigg, to investigate
    the contentious camps. They were phased out shortly after the committee submitted
    its interim report in February 1936. The last one closed June 30, 1936. Stone,
    Gladys May. Thesis. *The Regina Riot: 1935*. 1967. University of Saskatchewan Library.
    pp 114–116

11	The Rigg commissioners met with the Regina Board of Trade on December 10, 1935, then left for points west, despite unrest at the nearby Dundurn Camp. "Relief Camps Opposed by Regina Men. Board of Trade Members Discuss Dundurn's Future with Ottawa Investigators." *Regina Leader-Post*, December 11, 1935, 1

12	It was alleged that "outside agitators," had been at Dundurn for several weeks. Two were ejected and a strike was threatened. "Rigg Commission is turning around at Nelson, British Columbia to help deal with Situation. Strike is Rumoured" *Saskatoon Star-Phoenix*, December 14, 1935, 3

13	The "small protest group" was the Relief Camp Workers Union. "H. J. Higgins is on a list of members of the Relief Camp Workers Union." RCMP File, Report, May 14, 1936

14	The Rigg Commission came back to Regina at midnight December 14 to deal with unrest at the camp. The meetings Higgins describes were probably held December 15 and 16, 1935. "Dundurn Men Reject Inquiry Offer: Situation at Relief Camp Not Improved. 800 Strikers Refuse Offer of Ottawa Inquiry Commission," *Regina Leader-Post*, December 16, 1

15	The Rigg commissioners were still at the camp December 19 and Rigg "didn't know when they would be leaving." "Rigg Commission Still at Camp." *Regina Leader-Post*, December 19, 1935, 3

Chapter 5: Brought to our Knees

16	The RCMP opened Higgins's file in December 1935 when he was "identified as a 'radical' at the Dundurn Relief Camp and removed during the Rigg Commission visit." Report "submitted by A/Sgt. Usher under date of December 21, 1935, at the time Higgins was mixed up in the Dundurn Relief Camp trouble." RCMP File

17	Rain fell at Dundurn on December 21, 1935. The only other rainy day that month was December 12. Environment Canada, Historical Data, Dundurn, Saskatchewan, December 1935.

18	This paragraph is a comment made by Higgins quoted in a feature story. Murray Hogben, "The People's War," *Whig Standard Magazine,* January 10, 1981, 6

Chapter 6: Over the Pyrenees

19	Higgins wrote most of this chapter in 1939. The last ten paragraphs were gleaned from notes and audiotaped comments made by him in 1977-1980.

20 In August 1936, a Non-Intervention Agreement was supported by twenty-seven nations including Germany, Italy, and Soviet Russia (not Canada). Most enacted legislation making it illegal for their own citizens to fight in Spain, hence the need for volunteers to get there illegally.

21 Though Canada wasn't party to the Non-Intervention Agreement, it did pass a Foreign Enlistment Act in April 1937, intended to prevent Canadians from fighting in Spain.

22 Higgins's passport was issued September 16, 1937 "for the purpose of travelling to his home in England for a visit." RCMP File, Letter to RCMP Commissioner from Department of External Affairs Canada, December 11, 1940

23 Western democracies refused to help the Spanish government against General Franco's military coup. Britain, the United States, and Canada were led by men who admired Hitler and Mussolini. Anything on the left was seen as the "Red Menace." This extended to Spain's left-leaning government, which had only remnants of its army, no planes to speak of, and while they had control of navy ports on the Mediterranean, most of its ships were torpedoed by Mussolini's submarines.

    Franco had the support of landowners, the nobility, the Roman Catholic Church, and most of the military's generals. All were threatened by the government's socialist reforms—notably removal of education from control by the church and redistribution of land to peasants to rid Spain of its feudal landowner system. The democratically elected government was mostly comprised of social democrats, but also socialists, unionists, anarchists, and a small communist party. Those who supported Franco were referred to as Rebels, Fascists, and Nationalists. Those who supported the government were referred to as Republicans and Loyalists.

    Germany, Italy, and the Soviet Union openly ignored the Non-Intervention Agreement. From the beginning, Germany and Italy provided Franco with military support, including trained troops and the latest in aircraft, tanks, and other war machinery. Seeing an opportunity, the Soviets entered the fray soon after, but the Republicans' alliance with Stalin's Russia was a devil's bargain. They gave up most of Spain's gold reserves to pay for limited military support and antiquated war machinery left over from wars that had taken place decades earlier.

24 The Comintern (Communist International) recruited volunteers from around the world, routing them through Paris. Estimates vary, but roughly forty thousand volunteers, from close to forty countries, fought with the International Brigades. Some identified as communist but most, including Higgins, identified as anti-fascist.

25 Some early international volunteers were in Spain at the time of the coup and volunteered immediately, but most arrived by ship or crossed the border legally near Perpignan, France. By May 1937, after countries signed the Non-Intervention Agreement and passed foreign enlistment laws, France set up roadblocks. Soon after,

a group was smuggled by ship from Marseilles to Barcelona. The ship was torpedoed by Italian submarines, making that route too risky. After that, most climbed over the Pyrenees under cover of night after being checked out by Comintern organizers in Paris.

26   "Bill" is probably an alias for Robert Clunie, born in England in 1916, who gave his occupation as journalist. www.international-brigades.org.uk/the-volunteers

27   Robert Clunie (Ingles) and Harry J. Higgins (Canadiense) are on a list of fifty-nine volunteers who arrived in Spain October 21, 1937 via Massanet. Higgins says he was with a group of twenty, so it's likely they went over in three smaller groups, all on the same night. The arrivals that day included twenty-six Canadians, twenty-six English, four Palestinians, two Yugoslavians and one Frenchman. Joseph A. Ouellette is the only Canadian with a French name so he was probably the one who helped Higgins and the four others arriving from England, find the Paris recruiting station. RGASPI Fond 545, Opis 6, Delo 35, 153-154

28   Higgins was enrolled in the International Brigades October 28, 1937. CM Replica.

29   For an animated map showing Franco's rebels overtaking Spain day by day, google "Video Spanish Civil War every day." S&F Production has produced a very good one.

30   "Finnish-Canadians from Fort William and Port Arthur were the *majority* in the Machine Gun Company." William Beeching, *Canadian Volunteers Spain 1936-1939* (Regina: Canadian Plains Research Centre, University of Regina 1989), 58

31   Since the 1970s, several guesses have been made about the man on the gun. One guess was Oskar Huosianmaa. (There is also a cropped version of this photo which excludes two men, one on the right side and one on the left.) Higgins does not appear to be guessing, since in the late 1970s, he used similar pen marks pointing to his head in three other photos which were undeniably him. This marked photo is from Higgins's copy of: Victor Hoar with Mac Reynolds, *The Mackenzie-Papineau Battalion* Toronto: The Copp Clark Publishing Company. 1969, photo section

32   Close to 1,700 Canadians and recent immigrants to Canada volunteered for Spain. Over four hundred were killed or went missing in action. Michael Petrou, *Renegades: Canadians in the Spanish Civil War* (Vancouver, UBC Press, 2008), 3

33   Higgins was trained by the second battalion of instruction in Tarazona de la Mancha, near Albacete. Start date was November 1, 1937. RGASPI Higgins, p 3

34   It is possible that Higgins was transferred to the 15th Brigade's machine-gun unit on November 30, 1937, though no official records have been found. In later chapters, it is apparent that Higgins fought not only with the Mac-Pap machine-gun company but also with machine-gun units in the 15th Brigade and the 35th Division.

35   The Republican Offensive on Teruel opened on December 15, 1937, but the
      Mac-Paps didn't leave Mas de las Matas for Teruel until December 31. Victor Hoar
      with Mac Reynolds, *The Mackenzie-Papineau Battalion* (Toronto: The Copp Clark
      Publishing Company. 1969), 163

36   There is nothing in Higgins's papers indicating he wrote about the Battle of Teruel,
      possibly because it went missing when he sent his material out for typing. The
      Mac-Paps were sent into Teruel at the end of December 1937. However, his CM
      Replica shows him there from November 30, 1937 to February 12, 1938. The Battle
      of Teruel took place in mountainous country during one of the coldest winters on
      record. The snow was deep, the roads icy, and the situation perilous. Soldiers did
      not have warm clothing, and many suffered frostbite. Losses were heavy. Teruel is
      seen as the turning point in the war. Its strategic location, and ultimate capture,
      made the way clear for Franco to conquer the rest of Spain. There are understandable
      reasons for the sparse records of Republican soldiers in the Spanish Civil War, not
      least because Franco captured or destroyed them. However, Higgins's record seems
      particularly bereft.

37   No pay lists can be found for Higgins's first four months in Spain. (He mentions
      being first assigned to an English company so perhaps something will be found
      there.) For the fifteen months he was in Spain, he has been found on only six pay
      lists (March, May, July, September, November in 1938, and January 1939). The
      Mac-Pap pay list for March was found in Nationalist Archives in Salamanca; there
      because the Nationalists captured a lorry in Gandesa on April 2, 1938 with all the
      15th Brigade records. Notes in relevant chapters give citations for the other five.

38   Contrary to his CM *Replica*, Higgins was not at the Battle of Teruel for at least part
      of February. A document dated February 11, 1938, indicates he was at Officer
      Training School with the Tarazona Battalion of Instruction Company 1. RGASPI
      Fond 545, Opis 2, Delo 264, ll. 107

Chapter 7: At Any Cost

39   This chapter is the first half of a piece that Higgins wrote in 1977, "Surrounded by
      Fascists at the Aragon Front." It, in turn, is based on a shorter account he wrote in
      1939. LAC, Mackenzie-Papineau Battalion Collection, MG30, E173, Vol 1, File 16, H.
      J. Higgins

40   After Franco's strategic win at Teruel, he launched a blistering offensive at the
      Aragon front with support from Italy and Germany. The Republicans were hugely
      outnumbered by Mussolini's troops and vastly outgunned by Hitler's planes and war
      machinery. It was an impossible situation.

41   Higgins's CM Original has an entry signed by Edward Cecil-Smith, showing that he fought at Azuara, Caspe, Gandesa from February 25 to April 4, 1938. This period encompasses the Mac-Pap pull-back from Teruel, the chaos of the Aragon Retreats beginning March 9/10, a regrouping period in the latter part of March, and the second stage of the Retreats, March 31-April 4. There is also an entry in Higgins's CM Replica with different dates. It has him fighting at "Aragon: Caspe, Gandesa" from February 20 to April 2, 1938. Neither is entirely accurate. Higgins Collection

42   This sentence was added by Higgins's editor when a document surfaced in Russian Archives showing he'd been at Officer Training School in February 1938.

43   Higgins used "Dawsey," one of the surnames used by Owen D'Arcy. Variations included "Darci" and "Darcy." D'Arcy's actual name is used in the narrative. www.spanishcivilwar.ca/volunteers/owen-darcy

44   In his exit questionnaire, Higgins says he was "commended" by Captain Rafael Buch Brage for his actions. RGASPI Higgins, 3

45   Included in Higgins's personnel file is a report by Helge Meyer, a Canadian member of the 15th Brigade's Communist Party committee. Meyer wrote that Higgins "was extraordinarily brave during the big retreats." Alec Donaldson (British) and Pablo Rodriguez also signed the report. RGASPI Higgins, Attachment

Chapter 8: Surrounded by Fascists

46   This chapter is the second half of a piece Higgins wrote in 1977, "Surrounded by Fascists at the Aragon Front." The first three paragraphs are based on the end of a shorter account he wrote in 1939. LAC, Mackenzie-Papineau Battalion Collection, MG30, E173, Vol 1, File 16, Higgins, H. J.

47   According to his RCMP file, Higgins was "extremely well-built," which could explain how he had the strength to hang on to the gun.

48   "Jack Matthews" was possibly a Lincoln Battalion volunteer named Kopel Koplowitz, who used the name "Matthews." He served in the 15th Brigade as *Auto Park Intendente*, which translates as "manager of the auto park." www.alba-valb.org/volunteers/kopel-koplowitz

Chapter 9: The Crossroad

49   In 1939, Maurice Constant, was overseeing a book about the Mac-Paps, and asked Higgins in a handwritten note to "Tell us the story of the special m.g. outfit. There

were not many Canadians in it and there should be some good stories of the fighting, etc. MLC." This chapter is possibly a response to Constant's request, albeit written by Higgins in 1977. See also Chapter 14, *The Battle of the Ebro*. Letter from Friends of the Mackenzie-Papineau Battalion in Spain. Signed by M. L. Constant, Secretary of the Editorial Commission. April 22, 1939. Higgins Collection

50   Congruent with Higgins's account on page 59 in the previous chapter, Hoar wrote, "That evening the squad returned to its company to find, according to Higgins, 63 men left standing of the 130 who had gone into action earlier in the day. *For the remainder of this phase of the Retreats, Grenier's squad disappears among the files of brigades making their way east. They will appear again in the second phase, their numbers noticeably altered after three weeks of brutal combat.*" Victor Hoar with Mac Reynolds, *The Mackenzie-Papineau Battalion* (The Copp Clark Publishing Company, 1969), 178

51   Higgins marked the paragraph, quoted in the previous note, in his copy of the Hoar/Reynolds book. In the margin he wrote, "special assignment." In this chapter, Higgins writes about his "special assignment," having "disappeared" into the 15th Brigade's Machine Gun Unit. It is circa March 12, 1938. Ibid

52   The Spanish Republican Army had Army Corps at different fronts at different stages. The 5th Army Corps was at the Aragon Front in the northeast quadrant of Spain—so closest to where the international volunteers were arriving after crossing the Pyrenees. While most 5th Army divisions contained only Spanish brigades, its 35th Division had a Machine-Gun Brigade plus six brigades of international volunteers sorted by language, including the 15th Brigade which was English-speaking.

Chapter 10: Capture and Escape

53   During the chaos of the Retreats, countless soldiers were lost, killed, or captured by the enemy.

54   The battalions of the 15th Brigade were resting and regrouping at Batea from March 19 (or 20) through March 31.

55   Meteorological reports for Tivissa, a nearby village, show the only rain in March was on March 22, 23 and 24. Information from Oscar Saladie Borraz at the Ebro River Studies Centre via Anna Marti in Spain.

56   Bob Dyer was listed as missing in action on March 17, 1938. www.spanishcivilwar.ca/volunteers/robert-dyer

57   The hospital stay would have been a couple of days at most, and it was likely in Valencia. Higgins mentioned being hospitalized there once but no records have been found.

Chapter 11: Death of a Comrade

58   This chapter takes place during the second phase of the Retreats; March 31-April 4, 1938. Higgins wrote it in 1939, and revised it slightly in 1977. His own collection is missing the last few paragraphs of the 1939 account. His complete 1939 account is at Library and Archives Canada. LAC, Mackenzie-Papineau Battalion Collection, MG30, E173, Vol 1, File 16, Higgins, H. J.

59   This anecdote has been misattributed to Walter Hellund in: Victor Hoar with Mac Reynolds, The Mackenzie-Papineau Battalion (The Copp Clark Publishing Company, 1969), p 187

60   Higgins wrote two accounts of Stanley Henderson's death; one in 1939 and one in 1977. This is his 1939 account. Stanley Henderson was killed April 1, 1938. www. spanishcivilwar.ca/volunteers/william-stanley-henderson

61   The International Brigades spent the next four months away from the front. Few international volunteers were arriving by then so Spaniards as young as sixteen began to fill their ranks. At the same time, the Republican Army was planning a large-scale offensive.

Chapter 12: Special Training

62   Higgins CM Replica indicates he was hospitalized at Valls on April 2. No release date is recorded. In the previous chapter, Higgins says it was for ten days from April 3.

63   On his exit questionnaire, Higgins says he was hospitalized at Valls from April 3-29, 1938, that he was appointed Cabo on April 24, and that he attended Cabo School in May. RGASPI Higgins

64   "Government forces" is probably a reference to Spanish brigades in the 5th Army, though, by now, there were also many young Spanish men in the International Brigades.

65   As of April 30, 1938, the 5th Army Corps was renamed the 15th Army Corps.

66   Higgins is on a list of Mac-Pap personnel for May 1938, showing only 339 left in the Mackenzie-Papineau battalion, amongst them the following Spanish soldiers pertinent to Higgins's memoir; José Medina (teniente) and José Díaz (soldado). Higgins is listed as a cabo. RGASPI Opis 3, Delo 455 60th BN "Mac-Paps" Personnel May 1938

67   Higgins is also on the May 1938 Mac-Pap pay list. RGASPI 1938-Fond 545 023, Delo 55, II, 63x

68 Academic, Jorge Marco, at the University of Bath in England, read the manuscript and confirmed that, while Higgins was not in a guerilla unit, "For sure he was working on intelligence, but it is not clear whether he was doing this work in relation to the military activities of the 5th Army or related to broader intelligence activities." Email from Jorge Marco to Janette Higgins, April 24, 2019

69 The reason for Cecil-Smith's suggestion that Higgins move into headquarters becomes apparent in a letter Higgins wrote to a Mac-Pap veteran, Len Norris, in March 1978. Excerpts have been used in this chapter. Here it is in full— "...after I received special training, I was under orders of the 5th Army Corps and only Cecil-Smith knew about it. Before that I attended an officer's training school but the few that attended that training were not promoted to any rank for security reasons. There was a captain who seemed to know what area I was in at any given time and he received his orders regarding my movements from brigade headquarters. Do you remember a Captain José Medina? Or a Captain Braze (sic) Well they were the ones that gave me orders where a machine gun was needed. Most of the time I did not know where the hell I was! Villages had no names as far as I was concerned." Higgins Collection

70 Captain Rafael Buch Brage's obituary mentions he was a dynamiter with a guerilla unit in the fall of 1936. Dean Burrier Sanchis, "The Last US born Volunteer: Raphael Buch Brage 1915-2018," The Volunteer, March 4, 2019

71 Captain Brage's ALBA bio features a photo captioned: "Captain Rafael Brage, Servicio de Inteligencia Militar (SIM), XV Brigade, May 1938." www.alba-valb.org/volunteers/raphael-busch-brage

72 José Medina Lopez was a member of the UGT, a trade union affiliated with the Spanish Socialist Workers' Party. In December 1936, he entered "las Milicias de Vigilancia de Retaguardia" (rear-guard surveillance militias). From August 1937 to March 1938 he was in "la Brigada Especial." In March 1938, he was in DEIDE (intelligence) and from April 1938 until March 1939, he was with SIM or military intelligence. Fundacion Pablo Iglesias, PSOE Archives, Biografico 12795, medina-lopez-josé

73 José Díaz Artacho and Higgins are listed in close proximity on the Mac-Paps July 1938 pay list. RGASPI Fond 545, Opis 3, Delo 569, II. 231

74 José Díaz Artacho volunteered February 4, 1937 as a member of "Bon. Democratico Federal de Milicia Antifascista") and ES.37274.CDMH/DNSD. Centro Documental de la Memoria Historica, PARES, Ministry of Culture and Sport, Spain. Ficha de José Díaz Artacho. Secretaria, Fichero 15, D0016745

75 This anecdote is from a feature story about Higgins. Murray Hogben, "The People's War" Whig Standard Magazine, January 10, 1981

76 After Franco broke through to the Mediterranean in mid-April 1938, he continued widening the wedge separating Republican-held territory. The International Brigades were resting and training while the Spanish Army fought to hold the enemy back. One could reasonably speculate that some internationals in intelligence and guerilla units were sent into the fray, so it's conceivable that Higgins and José Díaz were fighting, despite the lack of official documentation.

Chapter 13: Enemy Spies

77 This chapter combines the beginning of Higgins's piece entitled, "Crossing the Ebro" with his full account of "Enemy Spy Agents."

78 Higgins's "special assignment," prior to training the battalion's machine-gun company in July, was possibly with the 35th Division. He is not on the Mac-Pap pay list for June 1938, and he mentioned in the previous chapter that he was with the Spanish army. He *is* on the Mac-Pap pay list for July 1938. It has been signed, indicating his pay was picked up in mid-August. RGASPI Fond 545, Opis 3, Delo 569, II. 231

79 Higgins indicates in his exit questionnaire that he was transferred to the 35th Division's Machine-Gun unit in July 1938. He cannot be found on any August pay lists. RGASPI Higgins, 3

80 Comments on an audiotape Higgins gave to a reporter for the Toronto Star: "There were other battles I was in during my periods away from the battalion that the Army Corps sent me to with the special machine gun squads behind enemy lines and with Spanish battalions. Before the end of the war, the Army Corps destroyed the material that could be used to pinpoint any internationals who were captured." *and* "I belonged to Special Machine Gun Squads. In fact, I headed it up after going to Officer's School and then I was given three units of machine guns to be in charge of." Higgins Collection: Audiotape recorded in 1980 for a Toronto Star newspaper reporter, Side A, Marker 409

Chapter 14: The Battle of the Ebro

81 In 1939, Maurice Constant, who was overseeing a book about the Mac-Paps, asked Higgins in a handwritten note to "Tell us the story of the special m.g. outfit. There were not many Canadians in it and there should be some good stories of the fighting, etc. MLC." This chapter relates events during Higgins's time with the 35th Division machine-gun units. See also Chapter 9, *The Crossroad*, when he

is leading one of the 15th Brigade's machine-gun units. Letter from Friends of the Mackenzie-Papineau Battalion in Spain. Signed by M. L. Constant, Secretary of the Editorial Commission. April 22, 1939. Higgins Collection

82 This description combines Higgins's brief 1977 version with audio-taped ad libs (1980) and other details he remembered when Manuel Alvarez found him.

83 Alvarez records the date of his rescue as July 28, 1938. Manuel Alvarez, *The Tall Soldier: My 40-year search for the Man Who Saved My Life* (Toronto: Virgo Press 1980), 223

84 Alec Wainman's son, having published a book of his father's long-lost photos in 2015, heard the story of Alvarez and Higgins in 2017, and realized this photo was of Alvarez. It's the only picture Wainman took of a wounded civilian in hospital. Serge Alternes and Alec Wainman, "Live Souls: Citizens and Volunteers of Civil War Spain," (Vancouver: Ronsdale Press, 2015), 238

85 Higgins indicates in his exit questionnaire that he was transferred to the 35th Division's Machine-Gun unit in July 1938. He cannot be found on any August pay lists. In this account, he is with the 35th Division helping a Spanish company move back. He also reports that he was at "Sargento School July 22 to Aug 26" (he probably meant Aug 22-26) and was "promoted to Sargento not confirmed." RGASPI Higgins, 3

86 This incident occurred circa September 13, since Higgins says later that he was hospitalized ten days after receiving the shrapnel wound. He was hospitalized September 23, 1938. RGASPI Higgins

87 Higgins's penciled account of his run-in with a communist "parade-ground" soldier (a swipe at someone who hasn't seen battle) has been inserted here. From the context, the incident happened September 21-23 when Spain's Prime Minister Negrin announced (September 21), and then withdrew (September 23), the International Brigades. Negrin hoped that, by so doing, Franco would ask Germany and Italy to withdraw support to the Nationalists. That did not happen.

88 In his exit questionnaire, Higgins reports being hospitalized at "Barcelona and Vich from Sep 23, 1938 till present date." This is approximately nine weeks in hospital/rehab for an infected shrapnel wound. It seems unlikely. More likely it was a cover for his staying on with the Republican Army after the internationals were withdrawn. RGASPI Higgins

89 Higgins is on the September 1938 pay list for the 35th Division's Machine-gun Battalion. There is a check mark in the receipt column, but no signature. All others signed for their pay. RGASPI F 545, Opis 3, Delo 16, 35th Division September 1938

90　Higgins is on a list showing him being paid at Vich for his September service with the 35th Division. This is signed, but it is not Higgins's signature. RGASPI F545, Opis 34, Delo 684, II, 201a Vich Militar No. 17

91　Comments on an audiotape Higgins gave to a reporter for the Toronto Star: "I was finally re-united with the special machine gun squads...this was only possible after being sent to the rear and being hospitalized a few days. In fact, it was only two days before I was taken to a rehab center in a convent that that been pressed into service and was being used as a rest hospital (rehabilitation) to help soldiers like myself to recover before being sent back to the units we belonged to." Higgins Collection: Audiotape recorded in 1980 for a Toronto Star newspaper reporter, Side A, Marker 409

92　This sentence is an ad lib Higgins made in 1977 when audiotaping "Enemy Spies." Higgins Collection, Tape 3, Side 2, Counter 525

93　In light of Franco's record of killing and imprisoning tens of thousands of known or suspected government supporters after the war, one wonders whether José Díaz Artacho would have survived. There is a brief record of him in the "political repression under Franco" section of the Spanish Archives. It records that he was a machine gunner, and that he volunteered February 4, 1937 as a member of "Bon. Democratico Federal de Milicia Antifascista") and ES.37274.CDMH/DNSD. Centro Documental de la Memoria Historica, PARES, Ministry of Culture and Sport, Spain. Ficha de José Díaz Artacho. Secretaria, Fichero 15, D0016745

94　Captain Rafael Buch Brage, one of Higgins's intelligence officers, escaped with Spanish refugees into France and found his way to Mexico. He returned to the United States on December 20, 1939, joined the British Intelligence Service in 1940, and fought with the United States when it entered the war. Brage returned to Spain with his family in 1954 and retired in France in the 1970s. He died alone and unknown in France on October 13, 2018. He was 103. Dean Burrier Sanchis, "The Last US born Volunteer: Raphael Buch Brage 1915-2038," The Volunteer, March 4, 2019

95　The intelligence officer Higgins was closest to, Captain José Medina Lopez, was captured at war end and sentenced to death. His sentence was commuted, and he was in prison until 1945, when he was released. He escaped into exile. He was with the Spanish Socialist Workers' Party (PSOE). Fundacion Pablo Iglesias, PSOE Archives, Biografico 12795, medina-lopez-josé

96　Higgins is on the Mac-Pap pay list for January 1939 at Ripoll, where the Canadians had been waiting for four months to leave Spain. There are no signatures. RGASPI Fond 545, Opis 3, Delo 774, II. 97

97   On January 26, 1939, Franco captured Barcelona. Most internationals had left earlier, but the Mac-Paps had been kept waiting in Ripoll, north of Barcelona, because of obstacles placed in the way by the Canadian government. Once removed, and private funds raised for their trip home, most Mac-Paps went to Cassa de la Selva and left Spain on January 26, travelling through France and England by sealed train. They boarded the Duchess of Richmond at Liverpool and arrived back in Canada February 3. Smaller groups made it home later in February. The Spanish Civil War was officially over April 1, 1939, when Madrid fell and what was left of Republican Spain surrendered.

98   Some internationals were prevented from returning to countries, including Canada, where they had been recent immigrants. They were sent back to their birth countries—regimes in Eastern Europe—put into concentration camps, and/ or executed. As well, thousands of desperate Spanish refugees streamed over the Pyrenees or along the road into France. Many ended up in filthy concentration camps on the beaches of southern France. Others went into exile. Still others fought in the French resistance. The international volunteers (and others) were right all along—Spain was Hitler's training ground—and World War II erupted a few months later. Franco kept Spain "neutral" in World War II, whilst currying favour with Hitler when it suited him. He was to remain dictator of Spain until his death in 1975. Spain transitioned to democracy, but decades later, her citizens are still coming to terms with the deep wounds wrought by their not-so-civil war.

99   The best-known parade occurred in Barcelona at the end of October 1938, when "La Pasionaria," Dolores Ibarrui, gave her renowned farewell to the International Brigades. There were others.

100   "I...can confirm...that *laissez-passers* did not in my experience generally have fingerprints on them, but then again, I don't think they were uncommon. From the pieces of information you have gathered it certainly seems like Jim could have been involved with some clandestine work for the Republic; the timing of absences seems to fit, especially the nine weeks convalescence for a relatively minor wound needing only two days in hospital, as well as his cryptic references. And some internationals certainly stayed on with Spanish units after the official farewell and formal repatriation in November 1938..." excerpted from an email to Janette Higgins, dated February 14, 2020, from James Matthews, Editor, Spain at War: Society, Culture and Mobilization 1936-1944. (London: Bloomsbury Academic. 2019)

101   The international volunteers' passports were stored at Albacete in the Republican region, cut off from where they were gathered near the French border to leave Spain. Without doubt, there would have been plans/attempts to smuggle them through enemy-held territory.

102   Higgins is on the Vich pay list for November 1938. He has signed for his pay.
RGASPI Fond 545, 03, Delo 692, II. 94a

Chapter 15: Heroes to the People

103   "Sons not with Party, Parents Sob as 10,000 Cheer for Mac-Paps," *Toronto Daily Star*,
February 6, 1939, 17

104   Victor Hoar with Mac Reynolds, The Mackenzie-Papineau Battalion (The Copp Clark
Publishing Company, 1969), photo section

105   Father R. H. Thomas was National Chairman of the Friends of the Mackenzie-Papineau
Battalion in Spain, the group responsible for raising funds for the rehabilitation of
returning veterans.

106   "James Higgins and Mike Sedor ... arrived home Tuesday afternoon (February 21)
at 3:30." They were met at the station by a hundred or more led by Rev W. G. Brown
before being taken to the Hungarian Hall where scores of people greeted them. They
were provided with an apartment at 319 Ave E South. "Spanish Veterans Greeted by
Crowd," *Saskatoon Star-Phoenix*, February 22, 1939, 4

107   A tag day was a popular way for people to raise funds for all sorts of causes. Donors
would get a tag on a string and hang it from a button on their clothing.

108   Saskatoon Mayor, Carl Niderost, claimed that Reverend Thomas was not a legitimate
member of the Church of England. In fact, he was an assistant with the Church of
St. Mary Magdalene (Church of England) on Manning Avenue in Toronto. Letter
from Thomas to Higgins March 4, 1939. Higgins Collection

109   A letter from Reverend Thomas to "Jim," dated March 4, 1939, stated that he
was "sorry to hear the Mac-Paps have become the victims of false propaganda in
Saskatoon." On March 21, Thomas copied Higgins on a letter in which he told
Niderost, "I also note that you received information from the Roman Catholic
Archbishop of Toronto which corroborated the testimony given by Mr. Higgins and
which you apparently withheld. I trust you will do what you can to make amends
and repair the unwarranted damage your equivocal remarks have caused." In an
accompanying letter to Higgins, Thomas said, "If you can get the Mayor to show you
my first letter, you will see he has deliberately chosen to misrepresent some of the
facts given there." Higgins Collection

110   From mid-February to mid-March 1939, newspaper accounts recorded the
controversy. Reverend W. G. Brown led a group, including Higgins, seeking city
approval for a tag day. Several representations were made. (Tag days were city
controlled to spread them out.) Mayor Niderost was adamant that Reverend Thomas

wasn't who he said he was, that the rehabilitation of returned Spanish vets was communist-backed, that he "saw little need for a tag day," and that the vets "would be given relief in the usual way." *Saskatoon Star-Phoenix*, February 24, 3; March 9, 3; March 10, 4; March 11, 3; March 14, 3

111   In response to an anonymous letter to the editor supporting the Mayor in his refusal to approve a tag day, Higgins wrote his own letter to the editor:

"After serving for many months in the Mackenzie-Papineau battalion in Spain, and having endured all the hardships and dangers of modern war, I can fully sympathize with the returned veterans of the Great War, and completely appreciate what many of them have had to face since they returned home.

"The people of Canada owe a great debt to the men who fought during the nightmare years of 1914-18. They went with bands playing and crowds cheering, sent by a Government to fight on foreign soil, in defence of Canada, who promised that nothing would be too good for its returned heroes. Where are most of these heroes now? Thousands are on relief; not living, just existing. For twenty years they have been fighting to improve these conditions and we as Canadians have stood by and watched, doing nothing to aid these men.

"The members of the committee, set up to help the boys that fought in Spain for the same reason that today the democratic countries of the world are uniting, are not standing by and watching. I wish now, Mr. Editor, to thank all those that have helped me and especially the boys who are not so fortunate as myself. I cannot understand why certain people go out of their way to try to stop this humanitarian work." Letter to the editor signed by H. J. Higgins, Saskatoon "From a Spanish Civil War Veteran," *Saskatoon Star-Phoenix*, March 25, 1939, 10

112   The tag day was held April 15, 1939, with the proviso that local citizens would manage it and any money collected would benefit Saskatoon men only. It raised $347.14. Jeff O'Brien, "It Happened 60 Years Ago!" *Currents*, City of Saskatoon Archives, Spring 1999

113   In late April, Higgins wrote at least one more letter to the editor concerning the plight of the unemployed. He ended it, "With all this war talk going on, I think the present Government should get down to brass tacks and start a war of its own; a war on poverty, unemployment and insecurity that would meet with the approval of the Canadian people. H. J. Higgins, Saskatoon. "How About a War on Poverty?" *Saskatoon Star-Phoenix*, April 29, 1939, 14

114   The United Reform Movement had its genesis in September 1938, when the Reverend W. G. Brown, already a leader in social justice issues, called together an informal group of fourteen people to discuss the reform of public affairs. After holding several meetings, they decided the best way to accomplish their goals was to "win the Saskatoon federal constituency in the next general election, and, to that

end, they solicited support from the C. C. F., the Communist Party, the Social Credit Party, and the Trades and Labour Council." Since Higgins worked closely with W. G. Brown when fundraising for SCW veterans, Brown would have been well aware of his capabilities and of their alignment on political issues. It seems that Higgins's many connections with those on the left—leaders as well as the rank-and-file— coupled with his independence, made him an ideal person to help Brown gain their support. Higgins doesn't mention the Social Credit party, perhaps because their leader was already on board—he was the one who nominated Brown at a public meeting held March 30th, 1939. J. M. Pitsula. "W. G. Brown: 'Righteousness Exalteth A Nation'" Saskatchewan History, Vol 33, No. 2 (Spring 1980), 56-70, quotation from 62

115   "The executive committee for the United Reform Movement is made up as follows; James Higgins (other names are redacted)." RCMP File, Report November 11, 1939

116   This group was probably the election campaign executive committee.

117   "Brown's personal charity, his interventions in the operations of the City Relief Office, and his speech-making on behalf of the homeless unemployed gave him first-hand knowledge of the Depression." For him "(t)he Depression had revealed the failure of capitalism, and the alternatives of communism and fascism beckoned." Brown had "some sympathy for communism" and admired their passionate commitment to the downtrodden, but his vision was of "a new social order based on co-operation," both in the "general sense of people helping each other" but also in business and politics. Pitsula. "W. G. Brown: 'Righteousness Exalteth A Nation,'" quoted phrases from 58, 59, 60

118   James Higgins...was on the leading committee subsequent to Brown's nomination on March 30, 1939. RCMP File, Report January 3, 1940

119   In writing his account of the "election" forty years later, Higgins blurred the distinction between an approaching federal election and a by-election which came first because of the death of the Liberal incumbent.

120   Reverend Brown was elected in a Saskatoon federal by-election on December 16th, 1939. He was to spend only one day in Parliament before it dissolved for the federal election on March 26, 1940. He won re-election but died on April 1. "The United Reform Movement in Saskatoon died with Reverend Brown. Without him, the movement lost its vital centre." Pitsula. "W. G. Brown: 'Righteousness Exalteth A Nation,'" quotation from 68

121   Janette Higgins has tried to determine the location of W. G. Brown's diary. She believes there will be mentions of Jim Higgins which pertain to his story. As of this book's publication, she has been unsuccessful. She would like to hear from anyone who has information.

122   This anecdote is adapted from a feature article about Higgins. Murray Hogben, "The People's War," *Whig Standard Magazine*, January 10, 1981

123   The Second World War started September 1, 1939 and the army immediately began recruiting in Saskatoon. "Major Roy McMullen Recruiting for Machine-gun Battalion," Saskatoon Star-Phoenix, September 7, 1939, 3

124   "James Higgins, who has been out threshing, has returned to Saskatoon. His future actions are not yet known but he may attempt to join the army." RCMP File, Report October 3, 1939

125   Higgins's RCMP file contains nineteen reports from February 1939 through May 1940. In addition, some of his correspondence was opened, transcribed, and kept in the file. Several reports indicate he could not be found in Saskatoon after May 1940.

126   In a loose note, Higgins mentioned that a friend who was superintendent of an apartment building gave him a spot to stay in the building's boiler room until the owner found out and "evicted" him. One could surmise that, by now, Higgins was being so harrassed by the RCMP that he felt the need to hide out. It was probably shortly after that he left Saskatoon.

Chapter 16: Over the Border on a Bike

127   On July 5, 1940, the following was reported: "Re James Higgins, Defence of Canada Regulations. On instructions of CIB Saskatoon accompanied by Saskatoon City Police, a search warrant was executed (July 2) at the house where Higgins was last reported to be living, 315 5th Avenue North. He was not living there and Mrs. Hill, the occupant of the house, said they had not seen Higgins for the past two months. He only visited and received some mail there." A note at the bottom says, "It is believed that James Higgins is at present on the Pacific Coast." RCMP File, Report, July 23, 1940

128   Janette Higgins remembers her father mentioning a girlfriend in New York named "Lilly." Found in his material was a book entitled, *All the Brave: Drawings of The Spanish War*, by Luis Quintanilla, with text by Elliot Paul and Jay Allen, and a preface by Ernest Hemingway. Modern Age Books. New York, 1939. It was inscribed, "To one who has endured much of what is in this book. I and many millions are trying to change it though. Through our defeats we'll arise victorious. Long live the Spanish people and the Loyalist Gov't." It was signed, "A comrade, Lillyan." Higgins added "1940."

129   Higgins's RCMP file contained letters from "Lillyan" addressed to him in Saskatoon before he left. The RCMP had apparently opened the envelopes, typed the contents

for Higgins's file, and put them back in the envelopes to be sent on to Higgins. He would have been well aware his mail was being intercepted. RCMP File 1939

130   This paragraph and the next were written by Janette Higgins with comment about hate excerpted from "A Statement about Fascism," written by Higgins in 1939. Higgins never did wrap up his story about the artist in New York; it trailed off into other stories, which in turn, opened up the floodgates of his memory for this book.

131   The border official may or may not have been sympathetic. There are no RCMP reports on Higgins's whereabouts after he left Saskatoon in May 1940. However, in April 1941, very shortly after he returned to Canada, Higgins's file indicates RCMP in Toronto were seeking his record from Saskatoon to ascertain if a James Higgins in Toronto was the same one who disappeared from Saskatoon. RCMP File, Intelligence Branch letter, Toronto, April 25, 1941

132   Paragraph written by Janette Higgins based on information in Higgins's RCMP file showing him working in Toronto from May 1941. He went off their radar in the Spring of 1942, but by July, the RCMP found him working in Peterborough at Canadian General Electric.

133   Higgins was "employed at E. L. Ruddy from March 26, 1941 until January 10, 1942 on outside sign painting...alleged to have conducted himself in a quiet manner and gave no reason for leaving his position there." RCMP File, Intelligence Branch, Toronto, August 21, 1942

Chapter 17: A Woman Like No Other

134   This chapter is adapted from a piece Higgins wrote privately for his children about their mother, which is why it doesn't include accounts of his union and political activities. It incorporates a bit from a letter he wrote to Reta before they were married.

135   Wartime houses were government-subsidized, one-and-a-half storey homes built to meet burgeoning housing needs in the 1940s.

136   This "nervous condition" is left unexplained. One wonders about post-traumatic stress disorder.

Epilogue: Secrets—But No Lies

137   Murray Hogben, "The People's War" *Whig Standard Magazine*, January 10, 1981

138   Ibid

139 "Higgins is about 35 years of age, about 5'6" or less, extremely well built, blue eyes, hair brushed straight back, thinning out at the front, thick lips, broad heavy nose. Wears a dark brown suit, blue work shirt." RCMP File, Report April 15, 1941, Note 6

140 RGASPI Higgins

141 Manley, John, "'Communists Love Canada': The Communist Party of Canada, the 'People' and the Popular Front, 1933-1939" *Journal of Canadian Studies*, Vol.36, Issue 4, 59-86

142 Report by Helge Meyer, a Canadian on the 15th Brigade's Communist Party committee. In the spot for "His general political attitude and the part which he has played in the political life is characterized by the following good qualities," Meyer has written, "Secretary of the Unemployed Movement in Saskatoon, Sask. In Spain, wall board editor for his company." RGASPI Higgins, Attachment

143 Victor Hoar with Mac Reynolds, The Mackenzie-Papineau Battalion (The Copp Clark Publishing Company, 1969), 238

144 William C. Beeching, Canadian Volunteers Spain 1936-1939 (Canadian Plains Research Center, University of Regina, 1989), Acknowledgements, xxxi

145 Based on Higgins's hand-written note (probably1977-80), here in full. "Although I wrote (1939) some of my memoirs of my activities in Spain, the material was not published. The reason being a book, that was being put together, was halted because the writers, who were gathering material from the vets, disagreed with the political editors. Cecil-Smith, who was the commander of the Mac-Pap Battalion during most of the time I spent in Spain, wrote to me of the problem. He suggested I should not send any more material for the proposed book until the problem was resolved. I am sorry that that problem was not resolved. The writers wanted to have the pros as well as the cons incorporated into the book, but the politicals wanted only the good points written. I recalled some of my own experiences that were not so good. In fact I was very close to being shot to death by a communist officer except for the intervention by a Canadian Corporal." Higgins Collection

146 The first book about the Mac-Paps was published in 1969. Higgins wrote on his copy, "Published too late by 30 years." Victor Hoar with Mac Reynolds, The Mackenzie-Papineau Battalion (The Copp Clark Publishing Company, 1969)

147 An RCMP report dated December 27, 1940 provides a brief overview of Higgins's activities from 1935 on, quoting from other reports that were purged from his file in 1972. It includes reference to a report of Higgins joining the Communist Party of Canada in 1937: "Item 3: A report submitted on July 17, 1937 under the caption "Communist Party of Canada, Saskatoon, Sask. Paragraph 3 reads: 'H. J. Higgins has joined the C.P. and is in their Unit 11.'" RCMP File, Royal Canadian Mounted Police, F Division, Saskatoon Sub/Division, December 27, 1940, 1

148   "J. Higgins and ..., two returned volunteers from Spain have resigned membership in the C.P. of C. feeling dissatisfied with the treatment accorded them by the C.P. of C. leaders in Saskatoon" RCMP File, Royal Canadian Mounted Police, F Division, May 21, 1939

149   Michael Petrou, *Renegades: Canadians in the Spanish Civil War* (Vancouver, UBC Press, 2008), 24

150   "Franco Dies. Higgins Lives. An unknown soldier recalls an all but forgotten war," *Peterborough Common Press*, November 25, 1975, 9

151   Duart Snow, "Writer's Search for heroic soldier ended happily after 40 years," *Ottawa Journal*, May 24, 1980, 61

152   Victor Paddy, "Tall soldiers still fight for recognition," *The Globe and Mail*, May 24, 1980, Entertainment, 3

INDEX

A SELECTIVE READING LIST

The Great Depression in Canada

Berton, Pierre. *The Great Depression: 1929-1939*. Toronto: Anchor Canada (a division of Penguin Random House), 2001

Broadfoot, Barry. *Ten Lost Years: 1929-1939*. Toronto: McClelland and Stewart, 1997

Liversedge, Ronald, Victor Hoar ed. *Recollections of the On-To-Ottawa Trek*. Toronto: McClelland and Stewart, 1973

Books by and about Canadians in the Spanish Civil War

Alvarez, Manuel. *The Tall Soldier: My 40-Year Search for the Man Who Saved my Life*. Vancouver: New Star Books, 1983

Beeching, William C. *Canadian Volunteers: Spain 1936-39*. Regina: Canadian Plains Research Center, 1989

Gouter, David. *A Chance to Fight Hitler, A Canadian Volunteer in the Spanish Civil War*. Toronto: Between the Lines, 2018

Hoar, Victor with Reynolds, Mac. *The Mackenzie-Papineau Battalion:* Toronto: The Copp Clark Publishing Company, 1969 (republished with a subtitle "The Canadian Contingent in the Spanish Civil War" by McGill-Queens University Press in 1987)

Liversedge, Ronald. David Yorke ed. *Mac-Pap: Memoir of a Canadian in the Spanish Civil War*. Vancouver: New Star Books, 2013

Petrou, Michael. *Renegades: Canadians in the Spanish Civil War*. Vancouver: UBC Press, 2008

Stevens, Douglas Patrick. *A Memoir of the Spanish Civil War*. Athabasca (Alberta): Athabasca University Press, 2000

Wentzell, Tyler. *Not for King or Country: Edward Cecil-Smith, The Communist Party of Canada, and the Spanish Civil War*. Toronto: University of Toronto Press, 2020

Zuehlke, Mark. *The Gallant Cause: Canadians in the Spanish Civil War 1936-1939*. Vancouver/Toronto: Whitecap Books, 1996

As well, watch for Tyler Wentzell's upcoming biography of William Krehm, a Canadian who served with the POUM Militia in Spain. POUM stood for Partido Obrero de Unificacion Marxista (The Workers' Party of Marxist Unification). It was with the POUM militia that George Orwell fought during the early days of the Spanish Civil War.

The Spanish Civil War

There are thousands of history books written about the SCW. A good start is:

Graham, Helen. *The Spanish Civil War: A Very Short Introduction*. Oxford: Oxford University Press, 2005

A few of my favourite literary works

Allan, Ted. *This Time a Better Earth: A Critical Edition edited and with an introduction by Bart Vautor*. Ottawa: University of Ottawa Press, 2015

Allende, Isabel. *A Long Petal of the Sea*. New York: Random House, 2020

Hochschild, Adam. *Spain in Our Hearts: Americans in the Spanish Civil War, 1936-1939*. Virginia: Mariner Books (division of Houghton, Mifflin Harcourt), 2017

McLain, Paula. *Love and Ruin*. New York: Ballantine Books, 2018

Sansom, C. J. *Winter in Madrid*. Toronto: Vintage Canada (a division of Penguin Random House Canada), 2014

Shulman, Aaron. *The Age of Disenchantments: The Epic Story of Spain's Most Notorious Literary Family and the Long Shadow of the Spanish Civil War*. New York: Ecco (imprint of HarperCollins), 2019

Webster, Jason. *Guerra: Living in the Shadows of the Spanish Civil War*. London: Black Swan (Penguin), 2007

AN ANIMATED MAP

For an informative moving map showing Franco's rebels overtaking Spain day by day, see S&F Production's YouTube video. It's easiest to find by googling, "video Spanish Civil War every day."

To see the progression of Franco's rebel forces during Jim Higgins's time in Spain, pause the animation on the following dates:

October 29, 1937	Jim Higgins arrives in Spain
April 2, 1938	End of the Republican's Aragon Offensive, more commonly known as the Retreats.
April 15, 1938	Franco's forces reach the Mediterranean, cutting what is left of Republican Spain in two.
July 25, 1938	The Battle of the Ebro begins. Jim rescues Manuel Alvarez on July 28.
September 21, 1938	Prime Minister Negrin announces the withdrawal of the International Brigades
January 25, 1939	Most members of the Mackenzie-Papineau Battalion, including Jim Higgins, leave Spain. They were gathered north of Barcelona near the French border. Some were left behind in prison camps or in cut-off Republican territory around Valencia. Some died, but others made it out later in February and March.
April 1, 1939	Franco declares victory. He ruled as dictator of Spain until his death in 1975.

...AND MORE

Janette Higgins is available for interviews, readings, book clubs, and school and university visits either in person or electronically. All enquiries, including rights, review copy requests, desk copies, or the archival resting place of Higgins's papers, should be emailed to her at jimhigginsmemoir@gmail.com

She can also be reached through www.janettehiggins.com or Facebook @jimhigginsmemoir

CPSIA information can be obtained
at www.ICGtesting.com
Printed in the USA
LVHW030758220421
685213LV00006B/1123